THE
ILLUSTRATED
ROOM

THE ILLUSTRATED ROOM

20th Century
Interior Design Rendering

Vilma Barr

Dani Antman
Contributing Editor

McGraw-Hill

New York   San Francisco   Washington, D.C.   Auckland   Bogotá
Caracas   Lisbon   London   Madrid   Mexico City   Milan
Montreal   New Delhi   San Juan   Singapore
Sydney   Tokyo   Toronto

Library of Congress Cataloging-in-Publication Data

Barr, Vilma.
  The illustrated room : 20th century interior design rendering /
Vilma Barr, Dani Antman.
     p. cm.
  Includes index.
  ISBN 0-07-006131-9
  1. Interior decoration rendering. 2. Interior decoration—
History—20th century. I. Antman, Dani. II. Title.
NK2113.5.B37   1997
729—dc21   97-10379
                                                      CIP

McGraw-Hill

A Division of The McGraw·Hill Companies

1 2 3 4 5 6 7 8 9 0   IIMP/IIMP   9 0 2 1 0 9 8 7

ISBN 0-07-006131-9

The sponsoring editor for this book was Wendy Lochner, the editing supervisor was Christina Palaia, and the production supervisor was Suzanne Rapcavage. It was set in Novarese Book by North Market Street Graphics.

Printed and bound by Printvision.

Cover Illustration: Living room, Easthampton, New York, 1988 (see Figure 9.7).
Illustrator: Nadim Racy, Ellen McCluskey Associates.

McGraw-Hill books are available at special quantity discounts to use as premiums and sales promotions, or for use in corporate training programs. For more information, please write to the Director of Special Sales, McGraw-Hill, 11 West 19th Street, New York, NY 10011. Or contact your local bookstore.

To two distinguished teachers:

Stanley Barrows (1914–1995),
who influenced generations of interior designers,

and

Buddy Leahy (1942–1991),
who advanced the art of interior rendering.

CONTENTS

Preface

The Illustrated Room chronicles the illustration of designs for interiors through the 10 decades of the twentieth century. In no other epoch has there been such a variety of styles, both of interior spaces and the drawing styles employed to depict them.

We did not embark on this book with the intent to show an example of every type of interior in every decade. Doubtless, several volumes would be required to accomplish such a goal. Rather, there is presented in the following pages a varied and visually stimulating collection of renderings, sketches, presentation drawings, elevations, vignettes, and room paintings—culled from several thousand submittals we received from all over the world.

From quick pen-and-ink sketches to complex computerized outputs, there is hardly one style in this book that resembles another. Drawings can communicate the personality of a space, the intent of the designer, and the talent of the illustrator far more effectively than can a photograph. Even the most skilled photographer is limited by the science of optics and the limitations of film. And, of course, a photograph cannot show a room before it assumes three real-time dimensions.

At the beginning of each chapter is an introduction that gives a brief overview of the important events and trends of the decade—social, economic, and political—to give readers a better understanding of the forces that shaped significant movements in art, architecture, and interior design. In many chapters, there are examples of designs that are very recognizable as belonging to a certain period of the century. In the same chapter, there may also be illustrations of rooms that are virtually timeless; they would seem as fresh and tasteful today as when they were created years ago.

We have occasionally exercised visual license in organizing the groupings of images so that page layouts present styles and artistic approaches that are complementary.

Within each chapter, the first group of illustrations is of residential spaces—entry areas, living rooms, dining rooms, kitchens, bedrooms, bathrooms, furniture and lighting, and decorative details. The second group of drawings is introduced by lobbies, and moves on to offices, restaurants and dining establishments, hotels, schools, museums, libraries, and churches, recreational facilities, retail stores, banks, industrial facilities, and specialty interiors.

Works by many of the century's leading architects, interiors specialists, and product designers are included. Readers can gather ideas for their own living or working spaces by comparing how professionals through the years have made rooms come alive with imaginative uses of color, form, distinctive furnishings, and unique accessories. For designers, it is hoped that *The Illustrated Room* will become a valued reference and source of concepts for their own projects.

Acknowledgments

Many designers, illustrators, and curators have been gracious and generous in contributing the interior renderings shown in our book and providing background information and technical data. Without the fine cooperation of the many professionals and organizations that supplied the drawings included here, we would not have been able to meet our original objective for *The Illustrated Room*: to show in one volume a broad representative selection of interior drawings that span the twentieth century.

We wish to gratefully acknowledge the following individuals:

The late Stanley Barrows whose encyclopedic knowledge of twentieth century interior design is integrated into the text. Joseph Braswell, ASID, who guided this book's focus and format. Albert Hadley, FASID, for his own wonderful drawings and for drawings from his personal collection. John Drews of McMillen Inc., for the hours spent delving into the firm's archives and organizing the wonderful examples shown throughout this book; and Elizabeth Sherrill of McMillen for her encouragement.

We wish to recognize Michael McCann, Thomas W. Schaller, Frank Costantino, John Blackwell, Rael Slutsky, Steve Oles, and Carlos Diniz for their continued interest and guidance. Alex Mitchell of Baker Furniture Company for providing the transparencies of John Braden's wonderful renderings of model rooms. Jeremiah Goodman, one of the world's most admired illustrators of interiors, for allowing us to share some of his remarkable work.

Our thanks to Kay E. Kuter, who helped us select examples from the Leo "K" Kuter collection of rare original drawings of film sets, now in the collection of the Academy of Motion Picture Arts and Sciences' Margaret Herrick Library. To Rachel Kaplan, who made the complex arrangements for us to visit several museums in Paris in order to obtain images for *The Illustrated Room*. To Michael Garber, our administrative assistant, for his deft handling of the myriad organizational tasks imposed by a book that was six-and-one-half years in the making.

To Glenn Barr, for his research in Vienna and photographs of numerous drawings used in Chaps. 1 and 2. To photographer Jay Rosenblatt, for producing uniformly high-quality transparencies of many vintage and contemporary maquettes, models, and original renderings reproduced throughout this book.

And to Wendy Lochner, our editor at McGraw-Hill, for her patience and guidance, and for believing in us and in *The Illustrated Room*.

Vilma Barr
Dani Antman
January, 1997

INTRODUCTION

The Illustrated Room brings together creativity in room design with the artistry, skills, and techniques required to illustrate it. Through the medium of drawing, the designer and the artist can clearly observe how the details and the intent of a room combine to form a cohesive, aesthetic space that serves the needs of the user.

The Illustrated Room presents an overview of representative interior design styles and visual interpretations from the 10 decades of our century. The drawings clearly express the uniqueness and quality of the illustrator's talent and the diversity of presentation techniques. They range from the bold concepts of the Vienna Secessionists to the complex computer-aided drawings of the past few years.

Rendering is arguably a twentieth-century art form. To render an interior is to depict it as it will look when completed and furnished, to show the owner and/or user of the space how the intended design will be carried out. An artwork that interprets a room after it has been furnished and accessorized is called a room painting.

The illustration of interior spaces while they were still in the conceptual phase was carried out during much of the first half of the century by the project's designer. Some of the most famous architects and designers of this century's early decades produced their own renderings. Design education included the development of excellent drafting skills combined with personal artistic styles. Expressive and exquisite renderings drawn by Josef Hoffmann, Otto Wagner, Stanford White, Frank Lloyd Wright, Joseph Urban, Adolf Loos, Ogden Codman, Jr., and others of this era are now in private collections or owned by leading museums.

Rendering Becomes a Profession

After World War II, many designers began to focus more on the myriad details involved with the creation and detailing of an interior, and less on producing the illustrations of the finished room or commercial space. To serve the design professions, specialists trained in design, art, and perspective drawing were retained by architectural and interiors firms. These renderers (also referred to as architectural illustrators or architectural perspectivists) have their own distinctive artistic styles and approaches to translating into two dimensions the mood and appeal of a three-dimensional space and the intent of its designer.

The room renderer has to convey the personality of the still-to-be-created interior. Expert renderers combine imagination, perspective drawing, familiarity with light and shadow, and a working knowledge of the materials utilized in buildings and interiors. They must be expert at perspective drawing techniques based on formalizing reality, starting with one stable vanishing point and horizon line. The art of the renderer develops over time: 5 to 10 years is typical of the amount of training and development needed to become professional in this discipline.

Renderers often work under very demanding time constraints. Deadlines are often stringent; fees have to be negotiated to reflect the estimated hours of time needed to complete the project within the budget and complexity of the design; changes to the design sometimes occur after the drawings have been approved and the renderer has already applied color to the base drawing.

The selection of light sources is in many instances left to the artist's discretion. Employing their own visual language, the drama, energy, sophistication, charm, or other attributes that the designer has conceived for the space must be clearly defined by the renderer. In essence, the drawing has to speak for the designer in a manner that all involved can comprehend. And, with all the typical project's imponderables and last-minute upsets, the final product still has to reflect the renderer's best efforts and highest standards for artistic accomplishment.

"The Renderer's Art: Interior Illustrators Share Their Ideas on Creativity, Inspiration, and Technique" forms the Addendum. It contains a summary of responses received from illustrators who were kind enough to answer our questionnaire when we began our research for the book. It is a revealing commentary on how illustrators work and how their style and artistic outlook has developed.

For us, it has been an exciting (and consuming) process to review and select works for the book produced by many of the century's leading architectural illustrators and renderers, architects, interiors specialists, and product designers. We hope that *The Illustrated Room* will become a valued reference for designers and for all who appreciate this most expressive art form.

THE
ILLUSTRATED
ROOM

CHAPTER ONE

1900 to 1909

As the twentieth century debuted, interest in interior design grew as the work of artists, collectors, and architects became published and known throughout Europe and America. The emerging technologies of photography and photo-reproduction depicted homes for city and country living. Travel and illustrated journals brought knowledge about room decor from many countries. *The Studio, Jugend, L'Art Decoratif, Ver Sacrum* and others were vital in disseminating ideas in Europe advanced by Viennese designer Josef Hoffmann and his colleagues; Charles Rennie Mackintosh and the "Glasgow Boys"; William Morris, Edwin Lutyens, and others in England; and Paul Poiret and Hector Guimard in Paris. *The House Beautiful* and *House & Garden* in the United States showed drawings and photos of interiors based upon the era's most popular style trends: Arts and Crafts, Art Nouveau, Olde English, and Colonial and Federal.

Antique collecting, which had previously been the preserve of the scholarly antiquarian, became increasingly widespread. Wealthy American industrialist-collectors, such as J. Pierpont Morgan, Henry Clay Frick, and John D. Rockefeller, commissioned Richard Morris Hunt and other leading architects of the era to design opulent residences in New York City, Newport, Rhode Island, and affluent suburbs of Philadelphia and Chicago, and to fill them with lavish furnishings and artworks.

In 1897, *The Decoration of Houses* was published, a book written by the then little-known novelist Edith Wharton and Ogden Codman Jr., the talented and tasteful Boston-born designer and illustrator. Their friendship and professional collaboration began when Mr. Codman was retained by Mrs. Wharton to design additions and create the interiors for the Wharton residences, including her homes in France.

Their book argued that domestic architecture and furnishings could be improved by the study of the best examples of the past. Good decoration, they reasoned, is concerned with "the fundamental things, not with veneers of style, but with house decoration as a branch of architecture."

An increasing consciousness and observation of nature paralleled the most important style in decoration of the decade—Art Nouveau, literally *new art*. The central and unique characteristic of the style lay in the use of a sinuous flowing line resembling waves, flames, or the tendrils of growing plants, and it was interpreted by such master designers and artisans as Louis Comfort Tiffany in the United States and Emil Gallé in France. Ornamentation, typically based on nature, was used freely, producing flowing curves of vines, leaves, and flowers. Outlines of birdlike forms were sometimes integrated into the designs.

Overall, Art Nouveau achieved only limited popularity, due primarily to the high costs of production and limited distribution. It peaked and then virtually disappeared before World War I. But a half-century later, it resurfaced as collectors discovered furnishings and especially decorative accessories of the period.

In contrast to the florid, "whiplash" curvilinear expression of French Art Nouveau, German and Austrian designers cultivated a more austere and essentially rectilinear aesthetic, balancing smaller areas of rich or intricate patterns with larger areas of plain surface. In spite of national characteristics, there is an extraordinary similarity in the feel of artists and architects working throughout Europe. The work of the members of the Vienna Secession is a variation on Art Nouveau, utilizing more rectilinear forms. Josef Hoffmann, Otto Wagner, Adolf Loos, and others of the Vienna Secession were designing everything from buildings to tableware.

The prophetic work of Frank Lloyd Wright and others of the Chicago school began to influence architects all over the world. Wright was considered the premier American *ensemblier*; for his clients, he would create totally integrated environments, lending his originality to furniture, vases, windows, fabrics, and place setting designs. Louis Sullivan, the brilliant and enigmatic architect under whom Wright first trained, is credited as the creator of the modern skyscraper by employing steel as the structural frame instead of cast iron. He translated his philosophical ideas into a unique form of organic architecture marked by swirling motifs in metal used on the exterior and interior of his buildings.

The Arts and Crafts movement, a precursor to modernism, continued into the twentieth century. With the 1888 London exhibition organized by the Art Workers' Guild, the philosophical ideas and designs of John Ruskin, Charles Eastlake, and William Morris were more fully developed into furnishings and accessories. In the United States, the Arts and Crafts movement incorporated Japanese influences as well. Landmark structures of the genre such as the 1908 Gamble House in Pasadena by the architects Greene and Greene utilized indoor and outdoor terraces, verandas, and courtyards. In the New York City area, the architect Ernest G. W. Dietrich specialized in residences that were charmingly adapted Arts and Crafts concepts into designs that fit into suburban lifestyles.

Furniture maker Gustav Stickley marketed furniture in a modified "mission" style, based on Arts and Crafts silhouettes. Stickley believed that his designs were particularly suited to what he described as "the fundamental sturdiness and directness of the American point of view and the U.S. sense of individualism." To publicize his views, he founded the magazine, *The Craftsman*.

It was also an age of great public buildings—of town halls, hotels, theaters, and civic buildings of all kinds in America and Europe. The grand Beaux-Arts style, so-called because its source was the Ecole des Beaux-Arts in Paris, was often the style selected for such structures. McKim, Mead, and White (1879–1915) of New York City carried out many commissions for monumental classical buildings that contained great interior spaces. Architect-partner Stanford White was a brilliant, urbane, and multitalented designer with an unerring sense of style.

Otto Wagner, one of the acknowledged deans of the Viennese avant-garde, assembled an impressive portfolio of work that included public buildings; stations for the Stadtbahn, the early Viennese subway system; and apartment houses which he both developed and designed. He produced beautiful architectural drawings which were frequently exhibited for their artistic excellence.

In 1901, a year after the Paris Exposition Universelle had presented Art Nouveau at its apogee, a group of French designers formed the Société des Artistes Décorateurs. Their regular exhibitions for more than 40 years focused public attention on the work of emerging and established French and continental designers and craftspeople.

This simple and elegant line drawing of the entry to the Gamble House shows a Westernized version of the Arts and Crafts movement. The clean lines indicate the complexity of the decorative woodwork designed for the foyer and staircase. Dotted lines are used to indicate the patterns on the area rug, a technique repeated as the drawing's border.

The brothers Charles Sumner and Henry Mather Greene designed windows, skylights, lamps, and light fixtures using glass and metal that were adaptations of craft patterns. The Gamble House is now a museum. (*Courtesy of John Kyrk.*)

FIGURE 1.1   **Entry, David Gamble House, Pasadena, California, 1908.**
Design: Greene and Greene; *Illustrator*: Bill Hersey; *Medium*: Pen-and-ink

Architect and interior designer Ogden Codman Jr. produced beautiful classically rendered elevations. This flat elevation allows the viewer to see through a pair of French doors to a courtyard enclosure on the right and the surrounding landscape on the left. Indications of light and shadow beneath the console and from the opposite wall that is reflected in the centered mirror add depth to the image. (*The Metropolitan Museum of Art, Gift of the Estate of Ogden Codman Jr., 1951, [51.644.77(17)].*)

FIGURE 1.2 **Wall design with a pair of doors, c. 1900.**

Design and illustration: Ogden Codman Jr.

Much of the drawing of interior spaces in this era was done in a black-and-white linear style using pen-and-ink or pencil. When color was used, the tones were muted and soft, and very often expressed with watercolor.

Figures 1.3 through 1.6 are formal architectural drawings that have been lightly tinted with color. The style of Figure 1.7 is freehand and loose.

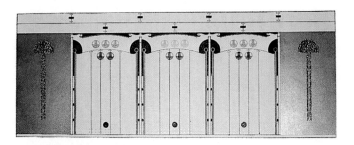

FIGURE 1.3 **Wall design for a foyer.**
(*Designer and illustrator unknown.*)
(*Das Interieur II, 1901, Library of the Universtädt von Bilding Künst, Vienna.*)

FIGURE 1.4 **Studies for the design and wall decoration of a hall.**
Design and illustration: Marcell Kammerer
(*Der Architekt X, 1904, Library of the Universtädt von Bilding Künst, Vienna.*)

FIGURE 1.5 **Design for a wall and pair of doors.**
(*Designer and illustrator unknown.*)
(*Das Interieur IV, 1903, Library of the Universtädt von Bilding Künst, Vienna.*)

FIGURE 1.6 **Entry hall.**
Design and illustration: Erich Nickel
(*Das Interieur III, 1902, Library of the Universtädt von Bilding Künst, Vienna.*)

Figure 1.7 **Study for a study and library.**

Design and illustration: F. Moro

(Das Interieur III, 1902, *Library of the Universtädt von Bilding Künst, Vienna.*)

Viennese architect Adolf Loos contrasted his sophisticated architectural concepts with a childlike, frenetic style of drawing and coloring. Loos spent three years in the United States and was influenced by Louis Sullivan and Frank Lloyd Wright.

Loos rejected ornamentation in favor of clean surfaces and functional furnishings. His sketches have an individualistic charm that emphasize his innovative use of surface planes. He was an expert at the complex ordering of interior space for his public and private commissions, and his drawings show his skill with the handling of rectangular planes. Loos also designed some products still in production, including Thonet bentwood furniture and Lobmeyr glasses.

FIGURE 1.8 **Entry hall.**
Design and illustration: Adolf Loos
(*Albertina Museum, Vienna.*)

FIGURE 1.9 **Entry hall.**
Design and illustration: Adolf Loos
(*Albertina Museum, Vienna.*)

FIGURE 1.10   Informal dining area.
Design and illustration: Adolf Loos
(*Albertina Museum, Vienna.*)

The Boston architectural firm of Shepley Rutan & Coolidge favored a linear architectural style for Figs. 1.11 and 1.12 that clearly shows both the basic design motifs and the applied decorative elements. According to a description of the Wightman house printed in a local newspaper of the day, the arched windows on the second floor were filled with colored glass. Below the central window on the main landing of the stairs was a large and elaborate pipe organ that could be played either from the landing or from the first floor living room. (*Courtesy of Shepley Bulfinch Richardson and Abbott.*)

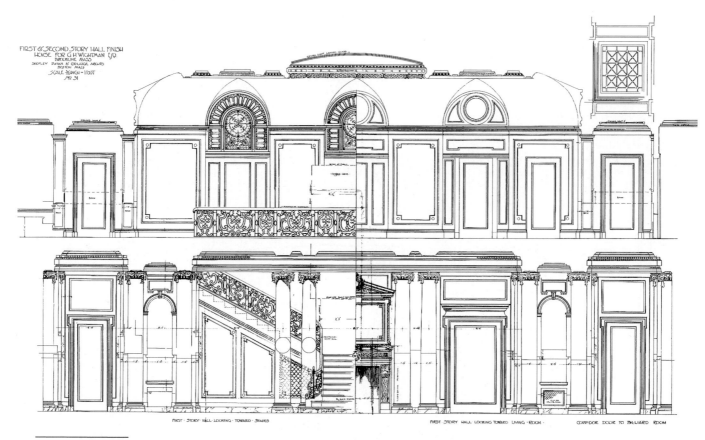

FIGURE 1.11   **Drawings for first- and second-story hallways, G. H. Wightman house, 1902, Brookline, Massachusetts.**

Design and illustration: Shepley Rutan & Coolidge Architects; *Medium:* Pen-and-ink

ORGAN
HOVSE FOR G.H.WIGHTMAN E/Q.
BROOKLINE MASS
SHEPLEY RUTAN & COOLIDGE ARCHTS
BOSTON MASS
SCALE ¾INCH = 1FOOT
№ 116

FIGURE 1.12   **Drawings for the organ, G. H. Wightman house, 1902, Brookline, Massachusetts.**
Design and illustration: Shepley Rutan & Coolidge Architects; *Medium*: Pen-and-ink

Tiffany, best known for his work in glass and metals in the Art Nouveau style, traveled to Europe in 1865 and was influenced by the Arts and Crafts movement. His design for the impressive entry to his own home reflects the exposed wood construction and high ceilings of a British country home.

FIGURE 1.13   Baronial Hall, Cold Spring Harbor, Long Island, New York, c. 1905.
Design and illustration: Louis Comfort Tiffany; *Medium*: Pen-and-ink

Figures 1-14 through 1-20 are examples of highly decorative individualistic designs by leading German and Austrian architects. They often emphasized their ideas by flat planes of vibrant color, balancing the impact of the strong color by leaving other areas in black and white to indicate that the design was still conceptual and not a finished room.

The presentation drawing by architect V. C. Mink for a house in Reingau adapts a wall design motif to side borders, an effective visual technique to integrate the interior design with graphic design for the print media popular in the early decades of the century. (Das Interieur III, 1900, *Library of the Universtädt von Bilding Künst, Vienna.*)

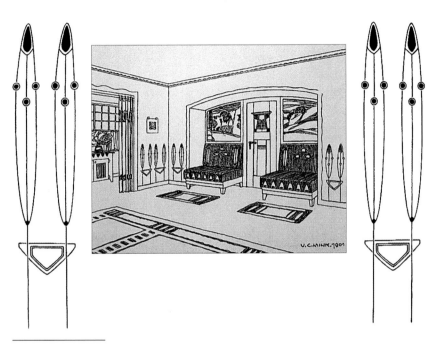

FIGURE 1.14   Concept for the living room of a country house in Reingau.
Design and illustration: V. C. Mink

FIGURE 1.15   **Room for a gentleman.**
Design and illustration: Max Benirschke
(Das Interieur IV, 1903, *Library of the Universtädt von Bilding Künst, Vienna.*)

FIGURE 1.16 **Design for a smoking room.**
Design and illustration: Max Benirschke
(Das Interieur IV, 1903, *Library of the Universtädt von Bilding Künst, Vienna.*)

FIGURE 1.17 **Study for a corner of a living room.**
Design and illustration: F. Moro
(Das Interieur III, 1902, *Library of the Universtädt von Bilding Künst, Vienna.*)

Intricate patterns on walls and furnishings combine with heavy texture on the floor to produce dazzling renderings by architect Josef Hoffmann and his contemporary, Leopold Bauer. On the rest of the drawings, color is flat and muted with areas left white to punch out the decorative design elements.

FIGURE 1.18 **Study for a student's room.**

Design and illustration: Josef Hoffmann

(Das Interieur I, 1900, *Library of the Universtädt von Bilding Künst, Vienna.*)

FIGURE 1.19 **Vignette with built-in seating.**

Design and illustration: Josef Hoffmann

(Das Interieur I, 1900, *Library of the Universtädt von Bilding Künst, Vienna.*)

FIGURE 1.20 **Reception area in a ladies' salon.**

Design and illustration: Leopold Bauer

(Das Interieur I, 1900, *Library of the Universtädt von Bilding Künst, Vienna.*)

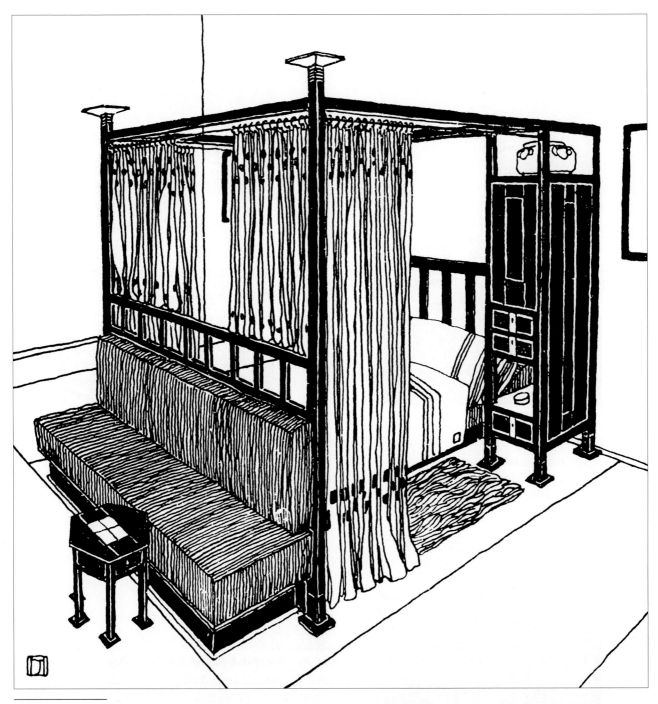

FIGURE 1.21   Design for a bed unit with storage chests, upholstered seating, and pull curtains on rods attached to overhead frame.

Design and illustration: Josef Hoffmann

(Das Interieur II, 1901, *Library of the Universtädt von Bilding Künst, Vienna.*)

Figures 1.22a to 1.22c are from an advertisement placed by The Globe-Wernicke Company.

Most advertisements in the early part of the century for home furnishings featured drawings. Photography and printing technology had not sufficiently advanced to give readers accurate representations of the room settings or products. Three drawings shown in Fig. 1.22 realistically and accurately render the mahogany and oak woods that were so predominate in furniture inspired by Arts and Crafts themes. (The Ladies' Home Journal, *November* 1906, *page* 64.)

FIGURE 1.22*a* Mission-style library.

FIGURE 1.22*b* Colonial-style living room.

FIGURE 1.22*c* Early English–style sitting room.

Figures 1.23 to 1.26 are designs and drawings by architect E. G. W. Dietrich.

New York architect Ernest G. W. Dietrich championed the Craftsman style based on the philosophies of visionary furniture designer Gustav Stickley. Mr. Dietrich's illustration style promotes a homey look with a lot of attention paid to the tools of everyday living. The wrinkles in the large rug in the foreground of Fig. 1.24 give a lived-in look to the wood-paneled living room. By contrast, the floor space in Figure 1.23 is depicted only by swirling lines, a technique that suggests atmosphere, texture, and gives visual interest to the drawing. Shadings are soft to blend with the rendering style. (*Courtesy of Riverow Bookshop, Oswego, New York.*)

Figure 1.23   **Library with fireplace and inglenook. Originally published in the May 1903 issue of *The Craftsman*.**

Media: Pen-and-ink with watercolor

Figure 1.24   **Living room with inglenook, brick fireplace, pottery, carpeted stairway, c. 1902.**

Medium: Watercolor on sketch paper

FIGURE 1.25 Arts and Crafts–style library, c. 1903, with built-in desk, stained glass windows, window seat, brick fireplace.
Media: Pen-and-ink with watercolor on sketch board

FIGURE 1.26 Bedroom with window seat, fabrics trimmed with Arts and Crafts–style designs.
Media: Pen-and-ink with watercolor on board

Figures 1.27 and 1.28 are interior perspective drawings of dining areas by architect E. G. W. Dietrich. Architect Dietrich produced timeless country dining settings. He rendered tile, wood, brick, glass, fabrics, and floor materials with an assured and communicative style.

FIGURE 1.27   **Tiled fireplace, paneling, window seat, fabric-draped trestle table, and Craftsman-style furniture, c. 1903.**
Media: Pen-and-ink with watercolor on sketch board

FIGURE 1.28   **Copper mantle over the fireplace, built-in cupboard, paneling, window seat, fabric-draped trestle table, period pottery, stained glass window, c. 1903.**
Media: Pen-and-ink with watercolor on sketch board

For the study in his own home, Stanford White produced this playful concept sketch of a dark oak sofa-back table with sculptural end piers. White maintained a residence in New York's Gramercy Park area, since demolished. His firm, McKim, Mead and White, was responsible for many of the late nineteenth and early twentieth century's outstanding structures, from the New York City Post Office to mansions in Newport, Rhode Island. (*The Stanford White Collection of Architectural Drawings, Avery Library, Columbia University, New York City.*)

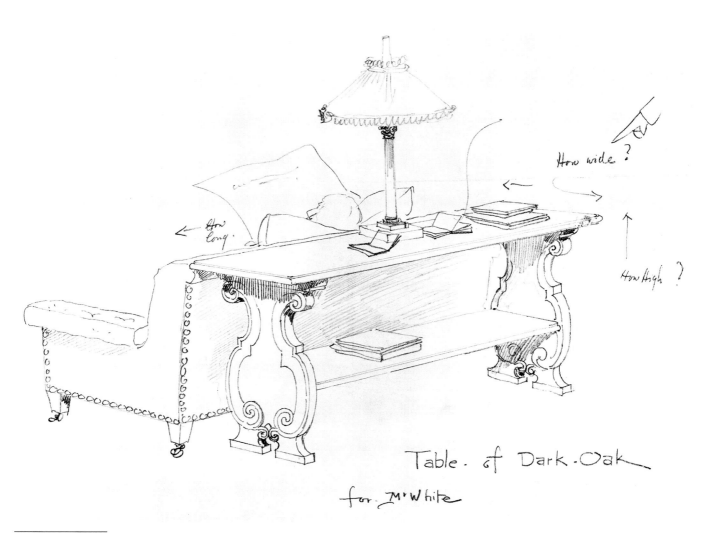

FIGURE 1.29 **Drawing by architect Stanford White for a dark oak sofa-back table designed for his personal use, c. 1901.** *Medium*: Pencil on paper

Hunt and Hunt, the successor firm of famous American architect Richard Morris Hunt, established by his sons, created a section perspective of an intricate proposed design involving carved stone, leaded glass windows, and tapestries or wall murals. (*Prints and Drawings Collection*, *The Octagon Museum*, *The American Architectural Foundation*, Washington, D.C.)

FIGURE 1.30 **Elevation of a medieval-style wall with a fireplace, c. 1902.**
Design and illustration: Hunt & Hunt; *Medium*: Probably watercolor

Clever use of perspective leads the viewer into and through successive spaces in Fig. 1.31. The figure of a black-and-white uniformed server in the doorway emphasizes both proportion and distance. The vignette illustrated in Fig. 1.32 is divided in half with two distinctive focal points: the curved window treatment on the left and the softly colored sitting area on the right. (Das Interieur I, 1900, *Library of the Universtädt von Bilding Künst, Vienna*.)

FIGURE 1.31 **Kitchen, with view into dining room.**
Design and illustration: M. Janner; *Media*: Probably ink and watercolor

FIGURE 1.32 **Informal dining area.**
Design and illustration: M. Janner; *Media*: Probably ink and watercolor

Figures 1.33 and 1.34 are interiors for the yacht *Noma,* 1902.

In the days when a private yacht was a floating handcrafted mansion, the leading architects of the period expressed their creativity in nautical terms. For the yacht *Noma's* unusual stair rail detail, a change in the weight of lines in the drawing emphasizes the hand carvings. The renderer of the yacht's dining room added a humorous touch by visually inviting a swashbuckler into the scene.
(*Prints and Drawings Collection, The Octagon Museum, The American Architectural Foundation, Washington,* D.C.)

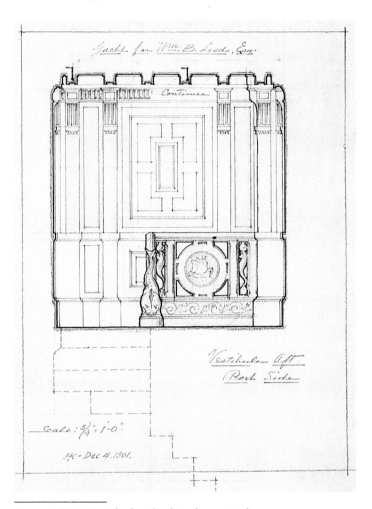

FIGURE 1.33   **Vestibule aft, detail, port side.**
Design and illustration: Hunt & Hunt; *Medium:* Probably pencil

FIGURE 1.34   **Dining room.**
Design and illustration: Hunt & Hunt; *Medium:* Probably pencil

Joseph Urban's swirling, romantic visual viewpoint is expressed in Figs. 1.35, 1.36, and 1.38 with his accented arches and strong perspective sight lines. Urban's illustrations show his attention to decorative detailing and his extraordinary technical drawing skills.

FIGURE 1.36   Main dining hall, Vienna.
Design and illustration: Joseph Urban; *Media:* Probably pen-and-ink and watercolor wash
(Das Interieur III, 1902, *Library of the Universtädt von Bilding Künst, Vienna.*)

FIGURE 1.35   Enclosed dining alcove, Vienna.
Design and illustration: Joseph Urban; *Media:* Probably pen-and-ink and watercolor wash
(Das Interieur III, 1902, *Library of the Universtädt von Bilding Künst, Vienna.*)

FIGURE 1.37   Drawing for a coffeehouse. Muted apricot and olive are typical colors of the era and are used here to offset the deep brown floor.
Design and illustration: V. Jerabce; *Medium:* Probably watercolor
(Das Interieur III, 1902, *Library of the Universtädt von Bilding Künst, Vienna.*)

FIGURE 1.38   Design for a large meeting room.
Design and illustration: Joseph Urban
(Das Interieur I, 1900, *Library of the Universtädt von Bilding Künst, Vienna.*)

Viennese architect Otto Wagner was an acclaimed urban planner and a developer as well as a master designer and gifted artist. His superb renderings often included fashionably dressed people who made the spaces he proposed seem realistic and lively. Here, he treats the whole page in his presentation, incorporating a border of sensuous flowing lines resembling natural twine, a surprising but fitting contrast to the image of the monumental public space it surrounds. Wagner employed an unusual perspective, midway between eye level and the underside of the balcony. (Der Architekt VIII, 1902, *Library of the Universtädt von Bilding Künst, Vienna.*)

FIGURE 1.39   **Central court for the proposed Kaiser Franz Josef Museum, Vienna.**
Design and illustration: Otto Wagner; *Medium*: Probably pen-and-ink

Cast bronze was specified for a reproduction of Gaudí's original chair. (*Courtesy of The J. Peterman Company.*)

FIGURE 1.40   Contemporary drawing of an armchair designed by Spanish architect Antoní Gaudí, c. 1902.
Medium: Gouache

Bright flat primary colors emphasize architectural planes and geometric patterns in these vignettes and furniture designs. Such drawings were produced for design journals that were read by both consumers and professionals.

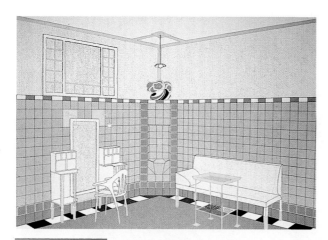

FIGURE 1.41   **Bathroom and dressing area.**
Design and illustration: J. Schwartz; *Media*: Probably ink with watercolor
(Das Interieur III, 1902, *Library of the Universtädt von Bilding Künst, Vienna.*)

FIGURE 1.42   **Armchair designs.**
Design and illustration: Hans Scharfen;
Media: Probably ink with watercolor
(Das Interieur IV, 1903, *Library of the Universtädt von Bilding Künst, Vienna.*)

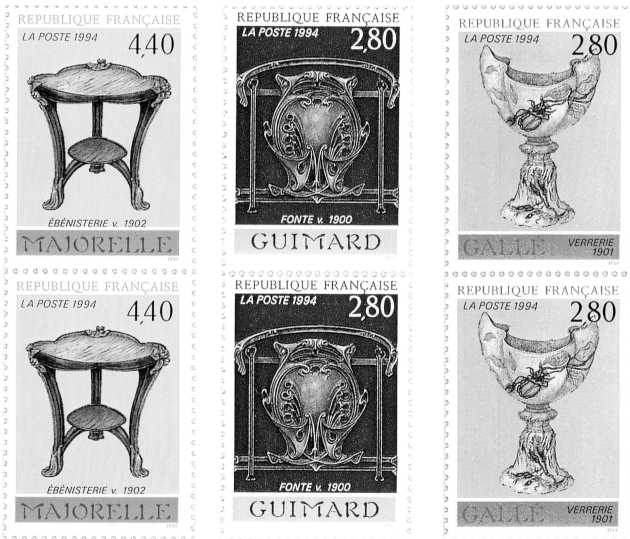

FIGURE 1.43 Group of contemporary French postage stamps depicting articles designed in the Art Nouveau style, c. 1900. Table, Louis Majorelle; teapot, Dalpayrat; ornamental cast metal, Hector Guimard; decorated glass footed bowl, Emil Gallé.

Before interior design came to be recognized as a separate profession, a building's architect often designed its important furnishings as well. These design development sketches were produced by Mr. Post for the suite occupied by the exchange's president.

Handwritten notes to the manufacturer describe specifications for the wood to be used, the dimensions, and general performance. "The dimensions of these chairs to be liberal and the utmost comfort is to be embodied in the finished chair," Mr. Post noted. The chairs were to be upholstered "with best horse hide supported on springs and best hair." Mr. Post's design for the front of the New York Stock Exchange building at 8 Broad Street is in the neoclassic style. (*Collection of The New-York Historical Society.*)

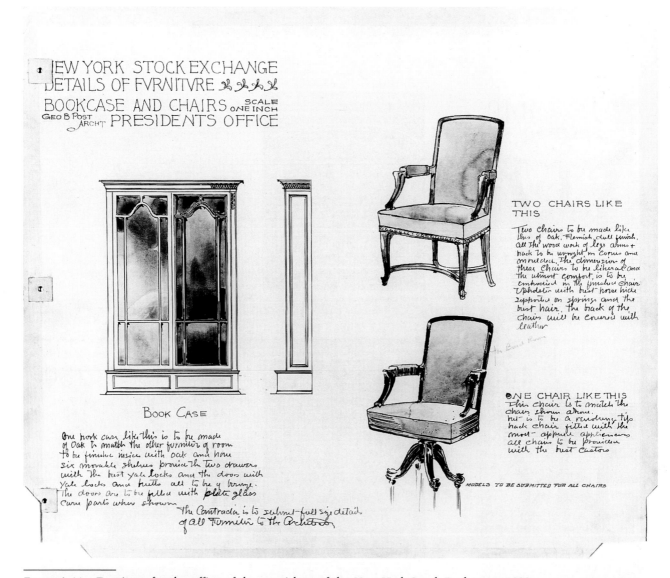

FIGURE 1.44 **Furniture for the office of the president of the New York Stock Exchange, 1902.**
Design and illustration: George B. Post; *Media*: Pen-and-ink and wash.

This one-point perspective sketch was likely a study drawing to evaluate the design of the staircase, based on the floor plan and elevations. It is a well-developed study drawing, giving architect Gilbert a visualization of the volumes within the space. A later version of this view would include color, surface, and light. The ornate ceiling is shown with the most detailing in this delineation.

Cass Gilbert (1859–1934) practiced during the era of eclecticism in American design. This interior has Italianate features; his Woolworth Building (Figs. 2.22 to 2.24) is neo-Gothic; one of his last works is the Supreme Court Building in Washington, D.C., a Roman Corinthian temple. (*Collection of The New-York Historical Society.*)

FIGURE 1.45   Grand staircase, Arkansas state capital building, 1909.

Design: Cass Gilbert; *Illustration*: F. G. Stickel; *Medium*: Probably pencil on mylar

CHAPTER TWO

1910 to 1919

An epoch's end was marked by World War I. Change—in economic relationships, in industrial production, in family living itself—was accelerating. Increasing power in the labor movement forced a shortening of the workday and increased leisure. Women took jobs in offices and factories. More people moved to the urban centers of the developed world, and the number of city dwellers increased markedly.

Influential designers who understood the impact of these new forces led the design movement into the modern era. Among the most prominent were Otto Wagner and Josef Hoffmann of Vienna; Charles Rennie Mackintosh of Glasgow; Walter Gropius, who first worked in Berlin; Swiss-born Charles Edouard Jeanneret (Le Corbusier), who relocated from his native Switzerland to live and work in France; and Frank Lloyd Wright and Louis Sullivan, both of whom began their careers in Chicago.

Hoffmann and Gropius applied their considerable entrepreneurial skills to establish design studios and manufacturing facilities to create and distribute products ranging from handcrafted jewelry to production-line furniture. Hoffmann in 1903 was one of the founders of the interdisciplinary Wiener Werkstätte (Vienna Workshop). He became the maestro of all that was fashionable in high Viennese taste and actively worked to blur the boundaries between the arts and between art and life. Walter Gropius founded the legendary Bauhaus in Weimar in 1919 to train artists and designers in the new theories of architecture, interior design, and related applied arts. It attracted some of the most creative minds of the 1920s, and contributed to the design of hundreds of two- and three-dimensional items: original works of fine art, photography, theatrical design, products for the home and office, as well as buildings and interiors.

Le Corbusier (1887–1965) was a prolific writer as well as a visionary architect. His treatise, *Towards a New Architecture*, argued for a theory of functionalism in design. Ornament was to be avoided, according to Le Corbusier, as a protest against applied decoration that concealed ill-planned buildings. He championed the adaptation of new forms of construction, such as reinforced concrete, and applied it at every opportunity. A prolific visual communicator, the complete collection of his drawings totals nearly 450,000 for designs ranging from housing to churches to government buildings in India. Several of his furniture pieces have become classics of modern design.

The multistory building was quickly moving from its original load-bearing structural system into the skyscraper category. Cass Gilbert's 60-story-high Woolworth Building in New York City was completed in 1913, and, at 760 feet, claimed the title as the world's tallest building. A steel-frame building, its exterior is modeled on medieval Gothic forms. The building's famous lobby is adorned with pseudo-Byzantine mosaics and gargoyles, some of which bear the faces of luminaries of the era, including his own image and that of his client, Frank Woolworth, among others.

Frank Lloyd Wright's influence achieved international status with the German publication in 1910 and 1911 of his Wasmuth Portfolio that detailed early Prairie-style houses. Wright believed that houses must closely relate to the outdoors, that windows are connections between nature and humans and that dividing houses into little unappetizing boxes was no longer valid.

"The Ideal of Beauty"
Frank Lloyd Wright with William C. Gannett

Can you buy taste? Taste cannot be manufactured. Like Solomon's "wisdom" it cannot be gotten for gold nor silver, be paid for the price thereof; but in house-furnishings, it is more precious than fine rubies. It is the one thing that no store in New York sells. Nor can rich relatives leave you any of it in their wills. And yet it comes largely by bequest. Nearly all one can tell about its origins is that it gathers slowly in the family's blood, and refines month by month . . . Taste shows itself in pictures, in flowers, in music, in the choice of colors for the walls and the floors, in the amenities of the mantel-piece and table, in the grouping of the furniture, in the droop of the curtains at the windows, in the way in which dishes glorify the table . . .

(*Courtesy of* The House Beautiful, 1896–1897, *The Auvergine Press, River Forest, Illinois; The Frank Lloyd Wright Fund.*)

The emerging profession of interior design in the United States was initially driven by the strong personalities and singular talents of women who introduced fresh ideas with panache and publicity. In New York, Elsie de Wolfe became a leading doyenne of the decorating world when she introduced light, air, white walls, and French-style accessories into interiors by stripping away the jumble of oriental carpets, dark window coverings, and heavy-framed paintings that were holdovers from the late Victorian and Edwardian eras. Ruby Ross Wood, who began her career with the *Ladies' Home Journal*, wrote Elsie de Wolfe's 1913 book, *The House in Good Taste*, and then published her own book, *The Honest House*. She favored designs inspired by eighteenth-century American and English antiques. Mrs. Wood ran the Au Quartième decorating shop in the John Wanamaker department store on Astor Place in New York with Nancy McClelland before establishing her own firm in the 1920s. Other notable New York women decorators of the decade were Rose Cummings, Mary Buell, and the Martini Studio. Frances Elkins, who designed interiors in the Midwest and California, combined European antiques with traditional Spanish features such as rough plasterwork, bare floorboards, and exposed beam ceilings.

The century's second decade is generally credited with ushering in the modern movement. A group of Dutch designers led by artists Piet Mondrian and Theo van Doesburg and designer Gerrit Rietveld adopted the same name as an influential magazine, *De Stijl*. Using primary colors with black, gray, and white, their works were studies in horizontal and vertical planes.

In Sweden, the country's modern design movement began with the 1917 Home Exhibition staged in Stockholm which introduced contemporary products to a new design-conscious working society. In Europe and the United States, mass production was established as the means for manufacturing and distributing products that were efficient, attractive, and affordable. Following the end of World War I, the growing desire to find better answers to the pressing questions of an industrialized society and human living accelerated the modern design movement.

Frank Lloyd Wright's exquisite sensitivity to form and functionality is apparent in this architectural drawing of a dining table and chairs produced for clients who retained his services to create their total living environment. Indications of a bowl and basket with cut flowers in Fig. 2.2 call subtle attention to the human details of the drawing and give proportion and composition. Wright carefully delineated the Japanese-style plant arrangement to complement his design of the taboret.

FIGURE 2.1 **Furniture details, dining room table and chairs, Henry J. Allen house, Wichita, Kansas, 1917.**
Design and illustration: Frank Lloyd Wright; *Medium*: Pencil
(Cooper-Hewitt Museum, New York City. Used with permission.)

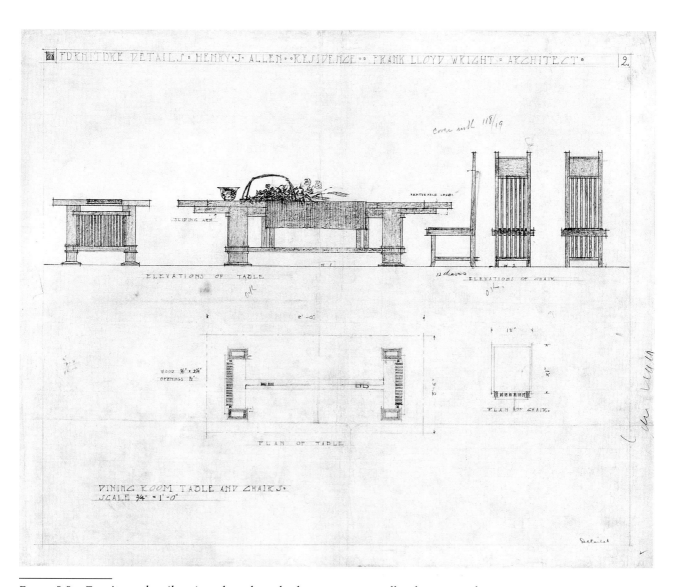

Figure 2.2   Furniture details, piano bench and taboret, Henry J. Allen house, Wichita, Kansas, 1917.
Design and illustration: Frank Lloyd Wright; *Media*: Pen-and-ink and crayon
(Cooper-Hewitt Museum, New York City. Used with permission.)

In Figs. 2.3 and 2.4, Jacques-Emile Ruhlmann used rich, earthy, vibrant colors to strongly delineate planes and the pieces of furniture of his own design. Ruhlmann was a reigning French interior and furniture designer, active until the early 1930s. His strong composition of overlapping forms of the view from the library into the living room is softened by a delicate indication of a casually draped transparent curtain.

FIGURE 2.3   **Vignette, entrance to a living room, c. 1913.**
Design and illustration: Jacques-Emile Ruhlmann; *Medium*: Probably opaque paint
(*Bibliothèque Forney, Paris.*)

FIGURE 2.4 **Living room, partial view, c. 1913.**
Design and illustration: Jacques-Emile Ruhlmann;
Medium: Probably opaque paint

(*Bibliothèque Forney, Paris.*)

Illustrator Pierre Brissaud could draw people and interiors with equal style and originality. His deft handling of this drawing room scene tells several stories simultaneously, posing the figures in the mannered mode of the era. Brissaud takes advantage of light emanating from lamps or sunshine through windows. His illuminated areas—on a wall, on an important section of the floor, or on

FIGURE 2.5   **Reception room, 1917.**
Illustrator: Pierre Brissaud; *Media*: Pen-and-ink and watercolor

some interesting piece of furniture—reveal every detail and yet do not throw the shaded areas into gloomy contrast. The use of rich colors on the furnishings of the room reflect the technique made popular for the famous stylized commercial posters of this period. (Gazette du Bon Ton, *Number 6, June 1914, plate 6. Collection of the author.*)

One of the country's leading home furnishings taste-makers, retailer W. & J. Sloane frequently employed artists to illustrate its merchandise and interior design services. The illustrator for this vignette used soft, muted pastel tones and lustrous highlights with edges fading into the background for a dramatic, atmospheric effect. (The House Beautiful, *February* 1917, *page* 122.)

Furnishings for a sitting room in designs that were suitable for export, according to a note on the original drawing.

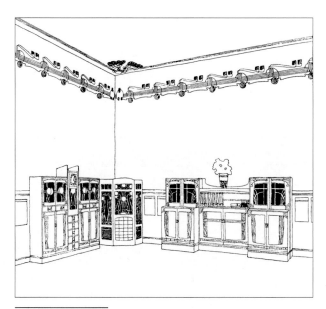

FIGURE 2.7   **Wall and corner cabinets, c. 1913.**
Design and illustration: Otto Prutscher;
Medium: Pen-and-ink

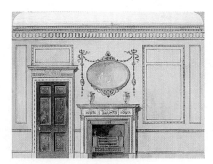

FIGURE 2.6   **Full-page advertisement placed by furniture retailer W. & J. Sloane.**
Medium: Probably conte crayon on paper

These three elevations (Figs. 2.8, 2.9, and 2.10) of fireplace walls are delicately colored. Architectural elements such as moldings and cornices are accurately detailed, while the portraits over the fireplace openings add a touch of pleasant realism to the drawings.

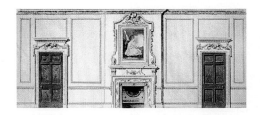

FIGURE 2.8   **Elevation of a wall with a fireplace in a dining room, c. 1915–1920.**
Design and illustration: Ernest L. Brothers for Litchfield & Company, London;
Media: Watercolor and pencil on paper, mounted on board
(*National Building Museum, Washington*, D.C.)

FIGURE 2.9   **Rendering of a wall with a fireplace for a small drawing room, c. 1915–1920.**
Design and illustration: Ernest L. Brothers for Litchfield & Company, London; *Media*: Watercolor and pencil on paper, mounted on board
(*National Building Museum, Washington*, D.C.)

FIGURE 2.10   **Rendering of a wood-paneled wall with a fireplace and built-in display cabinets, c. 1915–1920.**
Design and illustration: Ernest L. Brothers for Litchfield & Company, London; *Media*: Watercolor and pencil on paper, mounted on board
(*National Building Museum, Washington*, D.C.)

Early in his distinguished career, in the year when he moved from his native Switzerland to Paris, Le Corbusier produced this delightful scene with a sketchy, artistic hand. It is in a Romantic, rural style with variations on Art Nouveau themes, typical of the private homes he had designed during the previous decade, and before he turned to the austere and semiabstract style of his later works.

The flowing lines of the central curved staircase, the curved walls, and arched door frame give the space an architectural distinction, conveyed with his minimalist drawing style. Le Corbusier casually posed the male figure at a balcony railing, thus unifying the airy openness of the interior with the surrounding landscape. (*Fondation Le Corbusier. Used with permission,* ARS/SPADEM.)

VUE INTERIEURE DE LA GLORIETTE
SOUS LE RESERVOIR.

FIGURE 2.11   "Interieuer de la Gloriette Sous le Reservoir," Podensac, France, 1917.
Design and illustration: Le Corbusier; *Medium*: Pencil

Tiffany established his own studios in 1879 as Louis C. Tiffany & Associated Artists which offered interior design services, providing furniture, wallpaper, lamps, and his own stained glass designs. The Tiffany Glass Company was established in 1886 to produce vases, decorative items, and lamps, for which he gained international fame. This lamp was created for a client, Miss H. W. Perkins. (*The Metropolitan Museum of Art, Purchase, Walter Hoving and Julia T. Weld Gifts and Dodge Fund, 1967 (67.654.2).*)

FIGURE 2.12   **Drawing for a table lamp, 1915.**
Design and illustration: Louis Comfort Tiffany;
Medium: Watercolor and pencil on paper

French designer Jacques-Emile Ruhlmann expressed this bedroom/sitting room with an unusual blend of cool blues, mauve, and gold to communicate his concept for the integrated design of furniture and architecture. (*Bibliothèque Forney, Paris.*)

FIGURE 2.13   Bedroom, partial view, c. 1913.

Design and illustration: Jacques-Emile Ruhlmann; *Medium*: Opaque paint

Look closely at the patterns on the ceiling arches and the border above the arched wall openings. They are made up of the letters of the alphabet and are ingeniously used to create scale as they recede to the back of the library. (*Archives, Library of the Universtädt von Bilding Künst, Vienna.*)

FIGURE 2.14 **Study for a library in Leipzig, c. 1911.**
Design and illustration: Josef Hoffmann; *Media*: Pen-and-ink and wash

Architect Hoffmann cleverly gave viewers a visual signal of the intent of this space—a theater lobby—by including a partial view of a mural showing a softly rendered stage. (Der Architekt XVIII, 1912, *Library of the Universtädt von Bilding Künst, Vienna.*)

The visual drama of the theater's large curved wall is captured through the use of repetitive vertical lines and the overall composition. Color is used to separate the largest planes. (Der Architekt XVII, 1911, *Library of the Universtädt von Bilding Künst, Vienna.*)

FIGURE 2.15 **Study for a theater lobby in Kapfenberg.**
Design and illustration: Josef Hoffmann; *Media*: Pen-and-ink and wash

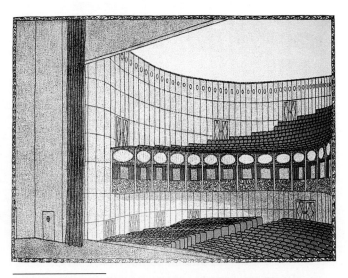

FIGURE 2.16 **Study for a theater as seen from the stage.**
Design and illustration: Josef Hoffmann; *Media*: Pen-and-ink and wash

FIGURE 2.17   Blue sitting room for Ivan S. Turgenev's play, A *Month in the Country*, 1917.
Design and illustration: Mstislav Doboujinsky; *Media*: Pencil and ink wash

FIGURE 2.18   Central court, proposal for the Vienna Stadtmuseum (city museum), 1912 (not built).

Design and illustration: Otto Wagner; *Media:* Pen-and-ink, colored ink, and gold leaf

Drawn in a grand and elegant style, this rendering elevates the department store to a monumental, near-cathedral status. Figures of people are presented as small blurs of movement. (*Photo, ©1994, The Art Institute of Chicago. All Rights Reserved.*)

FIGURE 2.19   **Perspective study of the interior atrium for Eaton's Department Store, Toronto, Canada, c. 1912.**

Design and illustration: D. H. Burnham and Company, Chicago;
Medium: Pencil on tracing paper

Figures 2.20 and 2.21 are the Woolworth Building, main street-level corridor, New York City, 1911–1912.

The 792-foot-high Woolworth Building was the world's tallest from 1913 to 1930 (it is now sixty-fifth). Located at 233 Broadway in the city's financial district, the 60-story building is covered by a neo-Gothic skin. The owner, Frank W. Woolworth of the five-and-dime store empire, who paid $13.5 million in cash for the building, favored the Gothic period for the company's headquarters. The elaborate lobby features marble, mosaics, stained glass, and gargoyles with recognizable faces, including those of architect Gilbert and Mr. Woolworth.

Gilbert's original concept drawing (Fig. 2.20) clearly depicts the strength of his design and the intended drama of the vaulted space with minimal but strong, dark gestural charcoal lines. The

FIGURE 2.20 **Design and illustration by architect Cass Gilbert.**
Media: Probably pencil and charcoal
(Collection of The New-York Historical Society.)

drawing is divided into three zones: the verticality of the walls, the curve of the vaulted ceiling, and the motion of the people at the ground level. Gilbert wanted to convey the dynamics of the building's proportions that visitors would experience—the upward thrust of the vertical pilasters in relation to the human scale and the arches of the vaults above.

Slashes of opaque white paint indicate light highlighting both people and interior surfaces, a contrast to the drawing's black tones and shades of gray. The drawing evokes an assurance and rapid expression of his talent and captures the architect's creative inspiration.

The fully rendered version (Fig. 2.21) shows the development of the ornate neo-Gothic detailing that makes the actual space so breathtaking. The viewer is led by the artist's detailing into the lobby's far reaches. The images of people are well-developed in their apparel and movement.

FIGURE 2.21   **Design by Cass Gilbert; illustration by T. R. Johnson.**

Medium: Probably pen-and-ink

(Collection of The New-York Historical Society.)

This rendering of the Woolworth Building's banking area is by one of the century's greatest architectural delineators, Hugh Ferriss, early in his career. The Ferriss style here generally adheres to the standards of high-quality architectural rendering of the period. He later became famous for dark, dramatic charcoal renderings that are more interpretive and sketchy (see Fig. 5.19).

FIGURE 2.22   **The Woolworth Building, banking area, New York City, 1912.**
Design: Cass Gilbert; *Illustration*: Hugh Ferriss; *Medium*: Pen-and-ink

Ferriss gave added distinction to Gilbert's landmark design with his own unique stylistic interpretation and flawless technique. He placed points of dark where his pen rested to keep the eye moving through the details of the drawing, introducing contrast to the line weight. People are expressed as outlines but still exhibit a great deal of gesture and character. (*Collection of The New-York Historical Society.*)

CHAPTER THREE

1920 to 1929

Released from the constraints of war, and buoyed by an economic boom, this decade saw an explosion of energy in the design disciplines. Various approaches to the "smart look," ranging from grand historical styles adapted to the smaller scale of modern life to avant-garde styles, were offered in the era's lifestyle publications.

A style based on new forms and materials was emerging on the Continent, grandly presenting itself in Paris in 1925. Art Deco (also referred to in America as Art Moderne) skillfully and artfully blended cubist and geometric forms, replacing the curves and sinuous shapes of Art Nouveau.

Several important salons staged during the 1920s showcased the important design movements of the decade, starting with the 1921 Paris Salon d'Autonne. But it was the 1925 Paris Exposition Internationale des Arts Décoratifs et Industriels Modernes that gave the multifaceted design style its name—*Art Deco*—and dramatically introduced it as the first total interior look to emphasize new technologies and materials. America was not represented at the 1925 Paris Exposition. Herbert Hoover, then the U.S. secretary of commerce, declined the exposition management's invitation to participate with the terse comment that there were no U.S. designers who could meet the organizer's specification for work which was of "new and really original inspiration."

Art Deco combined industrial design with such diverse elements as Japanese lacquer-work; African tribal art; stained glass; glittering exotic patterns on walls, floors, and screens; and contemporary abstract painting and sculpture. Variations on Art Deco's themes appeared in simpler, more practical furniture for smaller rooms in private homes and were adapted for theaters, hotels, and oceanliners. Such innovators as Jacques-Emile Ruhlmann, Eileen Gray, Süe et Mare, Jules Leleu, Maurice Defrêne, Paul Follot, Le Corbusier, René Lalique, and Charlotte Perriand contributed furniture, accessories, and whole environments that were coordinated from floor to ceiling, ashtray to chandelier.

Art Deco's polished, dynamic forms adapted well to contemporary tastes. The style is characterized by stepped forms, rounded corners, triple-striped decorative elements, and the use of chromium and black trim. From the beginning, Art Deco was commercially and fashion-oriented. It became a popular style for theaters, restaurants, hotels, oceanliners, and, in the next decade, for World's Fair exhibits and several notable skyscrapers, including New York City's Chrysler Building.

The discovery in 1922 of Tutankhamen's tomb inspired the Egyptomania of the decade. Symbols of papyri, lotus blossoms, and scarab beetles appeared in restaurants, lobbies, and theaters, and in jewelry, handbags, and other personal accessories.

The Bauhaus had relocated to Dessau, Germany. Geometric proportions that contributed to a unified look for furniture, ceramics, textiles, glass, and metalwork characterized the interiors produced by Bauhaus masters and students, utilizing materials such as tubular steel and Perspex, a clear plastic.

German architect Ludwig Mies van der Rohe was commissioned to design his homeland's pavilion for the 1929 Barcelona Exhibition. A generous budget permitted him to combine brass, marble, and expanses of plate glass. His elegant, sculptural leather-and-chrome Barcelona chair and stool are still in production.

Another architect whose furniture—tubular steel and glass tables and wood furniture—is manufactured today is Eileen Gray. She founded her own Paris decorative arts gallery in 1922 but soon changed her career path and became an architect, creating highly stylized residential interiors and signature furniture pieces.

Le Corbusier applied his theories of modern design to interiors. Collaborating on furniture design with Le Corbusier was the interiors specialist Charlotte Perriand. Two of their most notable pieces from their association in this period are the chaise lounge and sling armchair called "Gran Confort."

Streamlined and futuristic, products and interiors created by America's industrial designers—Raymond Loewy, Walter Dorwin Teague, Donald Deskey, Gilbert Rohde, Norman Bel Geddes, and Henry Dreyfuss—found growing favor with American consumers. Eliel Saarinen, who had emigrated from Scandinavia to the United States in 1923, was appointed director of the Cranbrook Academy of Art, Bloomfield Hills, Michigan. Interiors of his design were related stylistically to Northern Europe, utilizing light-hued furniture of clean, straight lines.

Prime examples of the European-inspired decorative arts movement were brought to American shores with the support of New York's Metropolitan Museum of Art and major department stores. In 1926, the Met organized the traveling loan exhibition, "A Selected Collection of Modern Decorative and Industrial Art," which featured over 400 items that were displayed at the Paris exhibition of 1925 and was exhibited at eight U.S. museums. The Met's hugely successful 1929 show, "The Architect and the Industrial Arts," had room settings by Raymond Hood, Eliel Saarinen, Eugene Schoen, and Joseph Urban, along with objects by 150 designers and craftspeople. R. H. Macy's 1927 Art-in-Trade Exposition had a "bring good art into the home" theme. Lord & Taylor's show was held in early 1928, with room settings that featured original works of art by painters Picasso, Braque, and Utrillo.

McMillen Inc., the first professional interior design firm in the United States, was founded in 1924 in New York by Eleanor McMillen Brown and is still a highly successful and much-admired design organization with an international clientele. Its ability and willingness to tackle interior architecture as well as decoration established its reputation and image as a major design resource.

By the close of the decade, other important interior designers that were serving residential and commercial clients were Thedlow, Tate & Hall, Elsie Cobb Wilson, and Margaret Owen in New York, and the brother-sister team of architect David Adler and interior designer Frances Elkins on the West Coast.

Theater design and movie set design were offering contemporary and period interiors as backdrops for dramatic and musical productions. Ziegfeld's famous Follies were visual fantasies, parading on stage a moving tableau of jewels, feathers, and sumptuous fabrics. Artists such as Erté designed dazzling sets for the shows that played to packed houses night after night. In Hollywood, movie set design was developing into its own discipline. Art directors worked closely with the film's directors to sketch out ideas for the scenes. Often, they used charcoal or pencil to produce a drawing right on the set, showing how the placement of the actors against the backdrops would ultimately appear on screen.

The Exposition Internationale des Arts Décoratifs et Industriels Modernes was presented by the Société des Artistes Décorateurs, a professional association of architects, artisans, and designers, founded in 1900. The pavilions represented four different viewpoints of the role of decorative arts. Le Corbusier's pavilion, L'Esprit Nouveau, emphasized, as he described it, "[equipping] a home with standard furnishings that are designed not for an *art* exhibit or a public accustomed to excess, but for industrial production, and that make no claims to an artistic character within a pretentious decor."

Prestigious French pavilions featured sumptuous interiors such as Hôtel du Collectionneur by Jacques-Emile Ruhlmann. The pavilion sponsored by the Musée d'Art Contemporain was more moderate in its approach to modern furnishings. Printemps and other major department stores sponsored pavilions. Exhibitors from other countries (although not the United States) were represented by pavilions and in the Grand Palais. The stylistic reference term *Art Deco* was adapted from the title of this exhibition. (*Collection, Museum of Modern Art, New York.*)

FIGURE 3.1   Poster commemorating the Exposition Internationale des Arts Décoratifs et Industriels Modernes, Paris, 1925.
Illustrator: Robert Bonfils; *Medium*: Lithograph (original size, 23½ × 15½ in.)

Leading French designers of the 1920s combined classic elegance, unusual materials, and high-style art to produce a sleek, urbane vocabulary of design. Jacques-Emile Ruhlmann and other innovators of the era contributed furniture, accessories, and whole environments that were unified statements of the designer's mastery of form and materials. For the trend-setting 1925 Exposition Internationale des Arts Décoratifs, Ruhlmann's dramatic rendition of a circular room, accented by the round carpet's circular pattern and the curved back of the desk chair, was one of the most admired of the model rooms on display. (*Bibliothèque Forney, Paris.*)

FIGURE 3.2   Petit Salon in the Hôtel du Collectionneur, Exposition Internationale des Arts Décoratifs, Paris, France, 1925.

Illustration and design: Jacques-Emile Ruhlmann; *Medium*: Opaque paint

Color and sheen are used in this advertisement to build demand for the flooring product. The illustrator showed bright sunlight streaming through a paned window onto a curved wall and curving staircase to contrast to the geometric two-tone pattern of the floor covering. (The House Beautiful, *January* 1928, *page* 7.)

FIGURE 3.3 **Illustration from a full-page advertisement placed by the Armstrong Cork Company, Linoleum Division.**

Design: Hazel Dell Brown; *Medium*: Probably watercolor

Color and drawing accurately reflect the components of modern living in the century's third decade. Although nearly 70 years has elapsed since these renderings were first published, we could feel at home in these rooms today with furnishings that can still be considered tasteful and contemporary.

Figures 3.4 to 3.9 are illustrations and designs for a study, living rooms, and an entry area. (1927. Decoration in Colour—100 Modern Interiors. *Stuttgart, Germany: Julius Hoffmann. Library of the Cooper-Hewitt Museum, New York City.*)

FIGURE 3.4   **R. Spaeth, Nürnberg.**
Medium: Watercolor

FIGURE 3.5   **F. Gebhard, Bremen.**
Medium: Watercolor

FIGURE 3.6   **W. Koch, Vienna.**
Medium: Watercolor

FIGURE 3.7   **H. Stierhof, Nürnberg.**
Medium: Watercolor

FIGURE 3.8   **L. Haas, Vienna.**
Medium: Watercolor

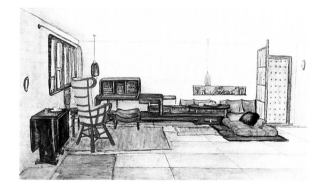

FIGURE 3.9   **K. A. Bicher, Vienna.**
Medium: Watercolor

In 1926, Grace Fakes joined McMillen Inc. which had been founded two years before as America's first professional interior design firm by Eleanor McMillen Brown. Ms. Fakes, with an encyclopedic knowledge of architectural details from classical periods to moderne, was also a talented draftsperson and renderer who remained with the firm for 35 years as its interior architectural expert.

Maquettes of proposed sitting rooms were rendered in watercolor to help the firm's clients imagine how the rooms would look when completed. New York City–based McMillen celebrated its seventieth successful year in business in 1994.

FIGURE 3.10 **Design by Grace Fakes, design director of McMillen Inc., New York City.**
Medium: Watercolor

FIGURE 3.11 **Design by Grace Fakes.**
Medium: Watercolor

From the text describing the drawings: "The chief characteristic of the French method of rendering, as evidenced by the drawings made in the studios of Carlhian of Paris, is their accuracy of line. All the designs shown here are accurate adaptations of the Louis XVI period of France in which the proportions, the detail and the ornament convey truly the spirit of the late eighteenth century." (The American Architect-The Architectural Review. *August 26, 1925, pages 183 and 184.*)

FIGURE 3.12 **Rendering by Carlhian of Paris.**
Media: Pen-and-ink and wash

FIGURE 3.13 **Rendering by Carlhian of Paris.**
Media: Pen-and-ink and wash

FIGURE 3.14 **Rendering by Carlhian of Paris.**
Media: Pen-and-ink and wash

Figures 3.15 to 3.19 are illustrations and designs for children's rooms and bedrooms. Three perspective techniques present different points of view for these rooms. (1927. Decoration in Colour—100 Modern Interiors. *Stuttgart, Germany: Julius Hoffmann. Library of the Cooper-Hewitt Museum, New York City.*)

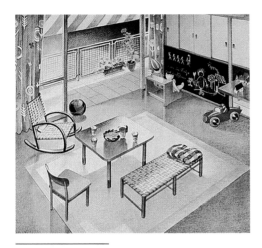

FIGURE 3.15   Perspective by R. Stotz, Bremen.
Medium: Watercolor

FIGURE 3.16   Single-point perspective applied by H. Bichler, Vienna.
Medium: Watercolor

FIGURE 3.17   A high-vanishing point applied by E. J. Margold, Berlin.
Medium: Watercolor

FIGURE 3.18   Single-point perspective applied by Hartig and Vöth, Mähr Schönberg.
Medium: Watercolor

FIGURE 3.19   Two-point perspective applied by H. Hartl, Essen.
Medium: Watercolor

Pen-and-ink and wash were used in this drawing of a baronial setting, a residence in Claymont, Delaware. Wash is made from ink that has been mixed with water. (The American Architect-The Architectural Review. June 18, 1924, *page* 62.)

The illustrator employed soft shadows from the wall-mounted sconces and the table lamps along with careful detailing of the screen, bookcase, and art to create an inviting residential setting. (The American Architect-The Architectural Review. June 18, 1924, *page* 49.)

FIGURE 3.20   Illustration from a full-page ad placed by The Welte Philharmonic Pipe Organ, Welte-Mignon Studios, New York City.
Medium: Pen-and-ink and wash

FIGURE 3.21   Illustrations from a full-page advertisement placed by the Lightolier Company.
Medium: Black-and-white gouache

Room portraitist Walter Gay and novelist Edith Wharton were close personal friends and both maintained homes in France. For her novel, *Ethan Frome*, Mr. Gay contributed a painting used for the frontispiece, his imagined version of the Frome's farmhouse kitchen. (*Wharton, Edith. 1922. Limited edition of* Ethan Frome. *New York, Charles Scribner's Sons. Frontispiece. Courtesy of Trina Duncan and Dr. Stuart Rose.*)

FIGURE 3.22   The "Ethan Frome Kitchen," Old Fairbanks House, Dedham, Massachusetts.
Artist: Walter Gay; *Medium*: Watercolor

Walter Gay (1856–1934) was a renowned room portraitist who painted rooms in famous homes in the United States and Europe. His painting of the Fragonard Room in the Fifth Avenue mansion of the industrialist Henry Clay Frick was interpreted in a light-drenched, soft-edged impressionist style that accurately captures the romantic mood of the eighteenth-century paintings by Jean Honoré Fragonard, around which the room was designed. (*The Clayton Corporation, Pittsburgh, Pennsylvania. Reproduced with the permission of the Frick Art Reference Library, New York City, reference no. 5327.*)

FIGURE 3.23   **The Fragonard Room, The Frick Collection, New York City.**
Artist: Walter Gay, 1928; *Medium*: Original, color oil

A generous budget allotted to the design and construction of the German pavilion at the 1929 Barcelona Exhibition permitted architect Ludwig Mies van der Rohe to create a jewel of a building that utilized brass, marble, and expanses of plate glass. He also designed the furnishings which included the modern classic Barcelona chair and stool, still in production today.

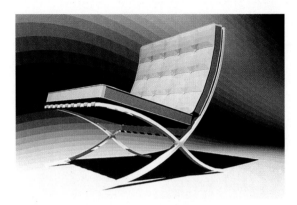

FIGURE 3.24   Leather and chrome chair originally designed by Ludwig Mies van der Rohe for the German Pavilion at the Barcelona Exhibition of 1929.

Illustrator: Skidmore, Owings & Merrill, Chicago; *Media*: Computer-aided design (executed in 1992)

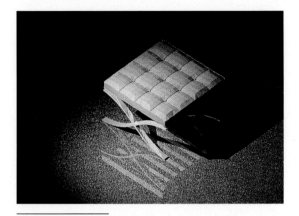

FIGURE 3.25   Leather and chrome footstool originally designed by Ludwig Mies van der Rohe for the German Pavilion at the Barcelona Exhibition of 1929.

Illustrator: Skidmore, Owings & Merrill, Chicago; *Media*: Computer-aided design (executed in 1992)

Figures 3.26 to 3.30 are sketches of modern classic furnishings designed in the 1920s.
Tubular steel furniture of the era is portrayed by sleek lines, influenced by the industrial age. Silhouettes are geometric, in the moderne style. (*Courtesy of The J. Peterman Company.*)

FIGURE 3.26   **Wassily chair, Marcel Breuer, 1925.**
Medium: Gouache

FIGURE 3.27   **Gran Confort chair, Le Corbusier, 1925.**
Medium: Gouache

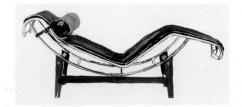

FIGURE 3.28   **Ville d'Avray chaise lounge, Le Corbusier, 1927.**
Medium: Gouache

FIGURE 3.29
Wagenfeld lamp, William Wagenfeld, 1924.
Medium: Gouache

FIGURE 3.30
Glass top table, Eileen Gray, 1927.
Medium: Gouache

American interior designer Ernest L. Brothers worked in England for Litchfield and Company and in Paris for Carlhian et Cie before opening his own firm in New York (see Figs. 2.8 to 2.10.) A talented artist, his evocative rendering of the draped fabrics lend depth to these elevations. Similar interpretations of traditional window treatments are currently being revived by designers using damask and other fabrics of earlier periods. (*National Building Museum, Washington*, D.C.)

FIGURE 3.31 **Drawing of draped bed by Ernest L. Brothers, c. 1920–1925.**

Medium: Watercolor and pencil on paper mounted on board

FIGURE 3.32 **Drawing of draped bed by Ernest L. Brothers, c. 1920–1925.**

Medium: Watercolor and pencil on paper mounted on board

FIGURE 3.33 **Drawing of window covering by Ernest L. Brothers, c. 1920–1925.**

Medium: Watercolor and pencil on paper mounted on board

FIGURE 3.34 **Drawing of window coverings by Ernest L. Brothers, c. 1920–1925.**

Medium: Watercolor and pencil on paper mounted on board

Figures 3.35 to 3.37 are interpretive concept sketches by Louis H. Sullivan, 1922.

Brilliant and enigmatic, Louis Sullivan (1856–1924) ranks as one of the most original of American design practitioners. Inspired by oriental art and by John Ruskin and Charles Darwin, Sullivan believed that decoration should relate to natural forms, and he translated his design philosophies into steel, a ductile material.

Sullivan's signature style was applied to building types ranging from the Carson Pirie Scott department store and the Auditorium Building in Chicago to community banks around the Midwest. For the swirling, complex designs shown here, Sullivan used pencil, a typical architect's drawing tool, to achieve an extraordinary fineness of detail. (*The Art Institute of Chicago, #1988.15.10, #1988.15.14, #1988.15.16. Photograph ©1993, The Art Institute of Chicago. All rights reserved.*)

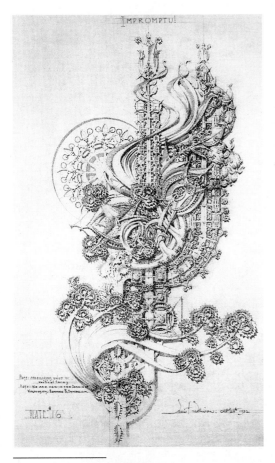

FIGURE 3.35   "Impromptu."
Medium: Pencil on Strathmore

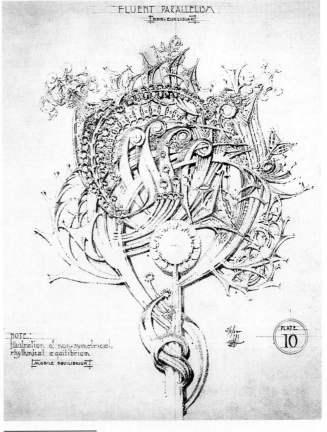

FIGURE 3.36   "Fluent Parallelism (Non-Eucludian)."
Medium: Pencil on Strathmore

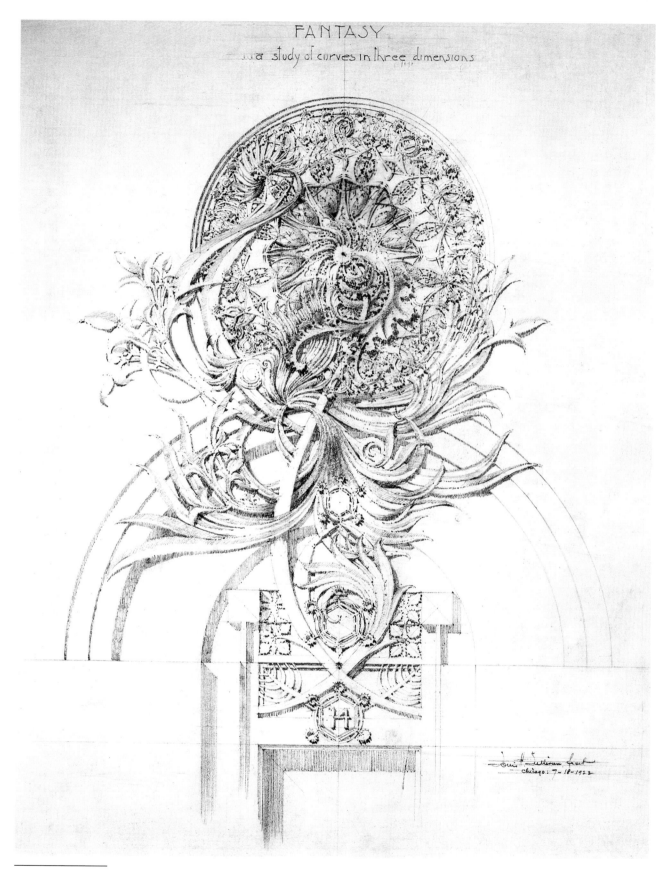

FIGURE 3.37 "Fantasy. A Study of Curves, in Three Dimensions."
Medium: Pencil on Strathmore

Multitalented Viennese-born Joseph Urban (1872–1933) created highly original interiors, products, graphic design, exhibits, and stage sets. From 1922 to 1924, he ran the New York City branch on Fifth Avenue of the Vienna-based Wiener Werkstätte and helped to popularize the European modern movement in the United States.

FIGURE 3.38   **Roof Garden of the Hotel Gibson, Cincinnati, Ohio, 1928.**
Design and illustration: Joseph Urban; *Media:* Pen-and-ink on tinted board with opaque white highlights

(*Cooper-Hewitt Museum, New York City.*)

A gifted illustrator, his distinctive design of a rooftop dinner theater features an intricate, tapestry-inspired wall and ceiling motif. Urban's flair for the theatrical was expressed in his stylized depiction of the diners and dancers, a 1920s version of Henri de Toulouse Lautrec's Paris cabaret posters of the 1870s.

The rendering of the palatial lobby of this world-class hotel was executed in black and white. Strong tonal contrast was employed for the polished black columns that stand out in relief against the light-tone walls and domed ceiling.

Decorative elements are suggestively rendered: the number of crystals on the chandelier is suggested and drawn as if the fixture is brightly lit. Carpet and fabric patterns are hinted, to be specified at a later date. People are placed at three strategic locations in the drawing, for scale, and to accent important interior design features. (*Restricted gift of Benefactors of Architecture, 1985.760. Photograph ©1994, The Art Institute of Chicago. All rights reserved.*)

FIGURE 3.39   Perspective view of the Empire-style entry to the Palmer House Hotel dining room, Chicago, Illinois, 1925.
Building design: Holabird and Roche, Chicago; *Interior design and illustration:* Mack, Jenney & Tyler; *Medium:* Watercolor on illustration board

Carrying out their client's objective to create a hotel where the guests would feel that they are in an undeniably important place, the architects and interior designers proposed a lobby conveying the effect of a European castle's main entry hall. The upward glow of lights from the candelabras and wall sconces onto the white stone walls draws attention to the ornate ceiling. For the elegantly dressed couple, their entrance is assuredly into a grand setting. (*Restricted gift of Benefactors of Architecture, 1985.762. Photograph ©1994, The Art Institute of Chicago. All rights reserved.*)

FIGURE 3.40 **Perspective view of the lobby, Palmer House Hotel, Chicago, Illinois, 1925.**
Building design: Holabird and Roche, Chicago; *Interior design and illustration*: Mack, Jenney & Tyler; *Medium*: Watercolor on illustration board; *Design*: Holabird and Roche, Chicago

These drawings were created by a European designer and artist, combining functional seating and work surfaces with fanciful applied ornamentation. The walls are intended to be bleached-grained wood panels. A mural on the wood paneling enlivens the elevation of the wall that forms a background for a deeply tufted, neutral color sofa.

Smooth, gradated washes complement the modern shapes of the furnishings depicted in these interiors. The upholstery covering for the desk chair, the sole dash of color in these twin renderings, is a rich orange hue.

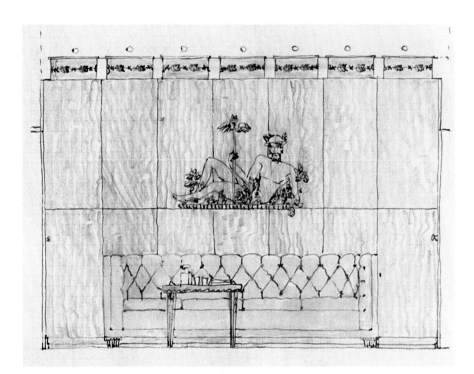

FIGURE 3.41   **Elevation for a private office.**
(Designer and illustrator unknown.)
Medium: Marker on grid paper

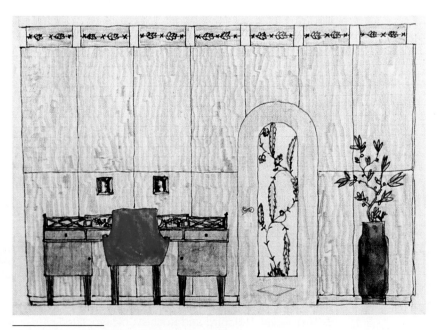

FIGURE 3.42   **Elevation for a private office.**
(Designer and illustrator unknown.) *Medium*: Marker on grid paper

Figures 3.43 to 3.46 are illustrations of designs for commercial uses, 1927.

For the second floor women's apparel shop in Fig. 3.46, the designer incorporated the facade of the facing building to give the feeling of a streetscape. The shop's name is prominent in script on the window; the large mannequin would be visible from the street. In Fig. 3.43, the attenuated wall mirrors provide contrast to the strong geometric shapes of the furniture and architectural elements. (1927. Decoration in Colour—100 Modern Interiors. *Stuttgart, Germany: Julius Hoffmann. Library of the Cooper-Hewitt Museum, New York City.*)

FIGURE 3.43   Hair salon, H. Becher, Elberfeld.
Medium: Watercolor

FIGURE 3.44   Dining room for a small steamer, K. Bertsch and A. Duetterle, Berlin.
Medium: Watercolor

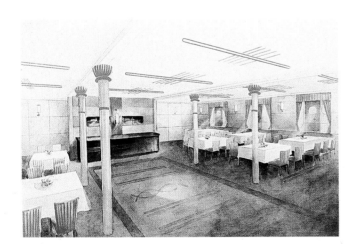

FIGURE 3.45   Restaurant, E. Fahrenkamp, Düsseldorf.
Medium: Watercolor

FIGURE 3.46   Retail store, R. L. Wendt, Berlin.
Medium: Watercolor

Leo "K" Kuter, one of Hollywood's pioneer art directors, amassed a comprehensive private collection of drawings and photos of movie sets and other movie memorabilia. His sketches, and those of the other great art directors of Hollywood's Golden Age, were quick visual memos to film directors. Most of the drawings were produced in pencil, charcoal, and china white; some were accented with color.

The perspective is that of a moviegoer, seated in a theater's central section. In these drawings, shafts of light are used pictorially to create drama for both movie sets.

FIGURE 3.47   Movie set of a Spanish-style loggia for *Rosita*, 1923. A Mary Pickford/United Artists film, Metro Studios. Ernest Lubitsch, director; William Cameron Menzies, art director; Leo "K" Kuter, supervising art director.

Illustrator: Leo "K" Kuter.

(Margaret Herrick Library, Leo "K" Kuter Collection, Academy Foundation, Beverly Hills, California. Courtesy of Kay E. Kuter.)

FIGURE 3.48   Nellie's dressing room, set for *The Monkey Talks*, 1927. A William Fox release of a Raoul Walsh Production, shot at the Fox Western Avenue Studios, starring Olive Burden and Jacques Lerner. Leo "K" Kuter, art director.

Illustrator: Leo "K" Kuter

(Margaret Herrick Library, Leo "K" Kuter Collection, Academy Foundation, Beverly Hills, California. Courtesy of Kay E. Kuter.)

Emblematic of the Roaring 20s were the sumptuous Ziegfeld Follies productions on Broadway. Early in his career, the Russian-French artist, Erté (born Romain de Tirtoff, 1892–1990), designed glittering stage sets for Ziegfeld's legendary chorines.

Here, he created a gold and black production number, positioning the bedecked beauties against a lavish backdrop. Erté's technique for this presentation drawing prepared for the impresario Ziegfeld's scrutiny and approval is flat and posterlike, reflecting the shape of the proscenium. (*The Pierpont Morgan Library, New York. Gift of Mrs. Donald M. Oenslager, 1982.75:204.*)

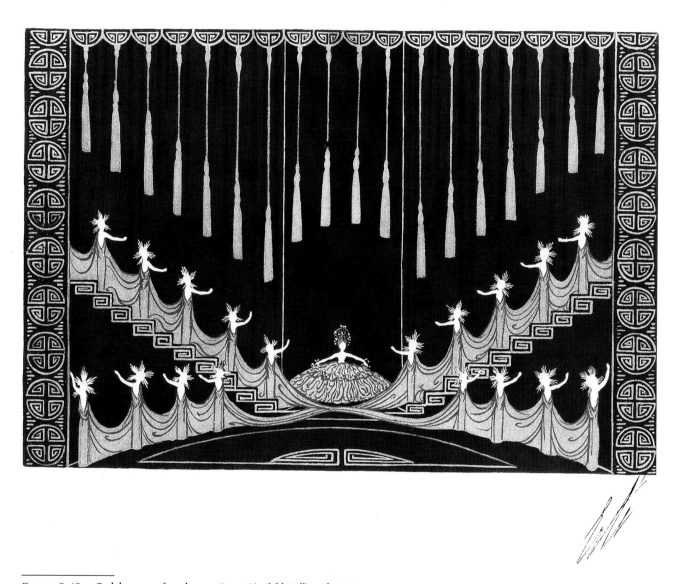

FIGURE 3.49 **Gold scene for the review, *Ziegfeld Follies of* 1923.**
Artist: Erté (Romain de Tirtoff); *Media:* Gouache and metallic paint

Tiffany elevated the decorative stained glass window to a status position for both residential and commercial use. He became the preeminent U.S. interpreter of the Art Nouveau style, with its free-flowing whiplash or "S-curves," based on forms found in nature. The retail store chain was founded by his father, Charles. (*The Metropolitan Museum of Art, Transferred from Archives,* 1958 (58.658).)

FIGURE 3.50   **Towle windows, Boston, Massachusetts, 1923.**
Design and illustration: Lewis Comfort Tiffany; *Medium:* Watercolor over black ink and graphite

CHAPTER FOUR

1930 to 1939

Beset by worldwide economic pressures, the 1930s were characterized by austerity in some countries, upheaval in others. In design, the acceptance of modernism grew, enhanced by the use of lacquer, mirror, cork, and the expertise of Scandinavian cabinetmakers with blond, laminated, and bent woods.

International Style was coined for the 1932 milestone New York Museum of Modern Art exhibit organized by Philip Johnson and Henry-Russell Hitchcock. The museum's galleries were filled with exhibits that demonstrated how the concept of flexible internal space could be adapted to contemporary homes and apartments. Model rooms proclaimed an absence of applied decoration, their walls devoid of color. Books and plants were introduced as accessories.

The 1939–1940 New York World's Fair marshalled the services of the best design minds of the era. Television emerged from the electronics test laboratory to amaze visitors. Technology promised better things to come and was a tangible expression of ingenuity—particularly American. Chicago's Century of Progress (1933–1934) and San Francisco's Golden Gate International Exposition (1939) featured murals, sculpture, and technological displays, with room settings by such leading designers as Marcel Breuer, Paul T. Frankl, Kem Weber, and Gilbert Rohde. The 1934 Contemporary Industrial Art Fair in New York and the 1937 Paris Exposition International des Arts et Techniques drew large crowds.

In Virginia, the opening of the Rockefeller family–funded Williamsburg, Virginia, restoration focused attention on Colonial and Federal period designs and initiated the historic preservation movement. Copies of licensed Williamsburg pieces were sold in retail stores.

Among those active on the New York interior design scene in the 1930s were Frank Alvah Parsons (who founded the School of Fine and Applied Art in 1909, later to become the Parsons School of Design in 1941), Mrs. Henry ("Sister") Parish III, Elsie Cobb Wilson, Nancy McClelland, and Eleanor

McMillen Brown. Billy Baldwin began his career with Ruby Ross Wood and went on to become the "Dean of American Decorators." William Pahlmann's daring model rooms identified Lord & Taylor with the era's design leaders.

William M. Odom, Parsons' president from 1930 to 1942, established the Paris atelier of the school. Stanley Barrows, who became director of interior design at the Parsons School of Design and later at the Fashion Institute of Technology, was the last member of the school's staff to depart Paris for New York following the German occupation in 1939.

After the Bauhaus was shuttered in 1932 by the Nazi-controlled German government, many Bauhaus masters emigrated to the United States, including Walter Gropius, Marcel Breuer, Mies van der Rohe, and László Moholoy-Nagy. Viennese architects Rudolph M. Schindler and Richard Neutra resumed their practices in Southern California. Architect Eric Mendelsohn also settled in America. The prolific Viennese-born Joseph Urban created Broadway theatrical sets and several pavilions at the 1933 Chicago Century of Progress Exhibition.

Oceanliners such as the *Normandie*, the *Bremen*, and the *Oslofjord* were floating examples of the best of contemporary taste: Art Deco and Moderne blending form with function, aesthetics with efficiency.

America's world leadership with the skyscraper was a bright beacon on the depression-riddled urbanscape. New York City's Chrysler Building, Chanin Building, and the Empire State Building presented Art Deco motifs on a monumental scale. Inside, public spaces are resplendent in geometric shapes, glossy woods, and stylized floral motifs. For New York City's Radio City Music Hall, industrial designers Donald Deskey and Gilbert Rohde created the widely publicized and copied aluminum and plastic decor and furnishings.

Streamlining was adapted for kitchen tools, serving implements, and mass-produced furniture. Rounded corners and adaptations of the teardrop shape identify with this trend. Swept-back lines and aerodynamic shapes had a monopoly on automobile styling. Interiors of luxury cars were plush and carefully detailed.

Henry Dreyfuss designed not only the interiors for trains such as *The New Century* but the streamline-style steam engine for *The Twentieth Century Limited*. He later wrote two books that became the foundation for the field of study now known as ergonomics, *Designing for People* and *The Measure of Man*.

Movie theaters offered patrons a few hours to forget about the Depression and their personal problems. Set designers created outlandishly fanciful interiors for the musicals of Fred Astaire and Ginger Rogers, the comedies of Carole Lombard, and the dazzling sequences for director Busby Berkeley that still amaze movie buffs. Trendsetting movie set designers included MGM's Cedric Gibbons, and RKO's Van Ness Polglase and Joseph Platt, who worked on *Gone With the Wind* and *Rebecca*.

Considered one of the most influential designers of the first half of the century was the French creative genius, Jean-Michael Frank. Frank was a critic at the Parsons' French branch and developed what has become known as the *Parsons table*, basically four legs and a top.

Pacesetting English society decorator Mrs. Syrie Maugham became an icon for contemporary taste and 1930s chic with the publicizing of her "All-White Room." Influenced by the ideals of the modern movement and nontraditional expressions in the fine arts, leading residential interior designers began to develop a richness of environment based on elegance in contemporary taste and proportion rather than historical precedent and the amount of ornamentation.

Finnish architect Alvar Aalto applied curved lines for his buildings, interiors, furniture, and glassware and vases. His signature chairs and stools of bent-plywoods and laminates provided inspiration to Charles Eames and Eero Saarinen, among others.

Fallingwater, one of Frank Lloyd Wright's most celebrated buildings, was constructed from 1934 to 1937. Designed as a country home for business scion and arts patron Edgar Kaufmann at Bear Run near Pittsburgh, Wright placed dramatic concrete cantilevers over a rocky waterfall in a wooded, rural site. The home is now open to the public as a museum.

Van Day Truex had a distinguished design career as a teacher, interior designer, and later as design director of Tiffany's in the 1950s. A benefactor of the Metropolitan Museum of Art, he was also an accomplished artist. These two room portraits—one a vignette of a room in a New York City residence, the other of a grand European salon—convey their ambience in an elegant, painterly manner.

FIGURE 4.1   Vignette, New York City living room, c. 1935.
Artist: Van Day Truex; *Media*: Watercolor
(*Courtesy of John Pierrepont.*)

FIGURE 4.2   Villa Barbaro, Rome, Italy, c. 1930.
Artist: Van Day Truex; *Media*: Watercolor
(*Courtesy of Nicholas Pentecost.*)

Room portraitist Elizabeth Hoopes could interpret any decorating style with the same finesse, to capture a room's underlying structure and ultimate livability. Her seemingly loose technique requires great expertise and control, here utilizing a wet-paint-into-wet-paint brush technique. Her judicious use of white paper as highlights gives these paintings an inner glow.

FIGURE 4.4 **Living room, New York City, 1934.**
Design: McMillen Inc.; *Illustrator*: Elizabeth Hoopes;
Medium: Watercolor

FIGURE 4.3 **Music room, Washington, D.C., 1934.**
Design: McMillen Inc.;
Illustrator: Elizabeth Hoopes; *Medium*: Watercolor

With an encyclopedic knowledge of the history of architecture and furniture and a keen eye for contemporary trends, Grace Fakes became McMillen's design doyenne. Her exquisitely rendered elevations in the maquette format simulated a three-dimensional experience for residential and commercial spaces.

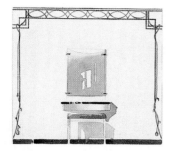

FIGURE 4.5 **Detail for a dressing room.**
Design and illustration: Grace Fakes for McMillen Inc.; *Medium:* Watercolor

FIGURE 4.6 **Detail for a dressing room.**
Design and illustration: Grace Fakes for McMillen Inc.; *Medium:* Watercolor

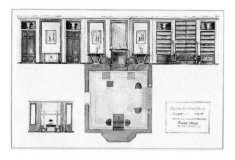

FIGURE 4.7 **Maquette for a small library, c. 1930s.**
Design and illustration: Grace Fakes for McMillen Inc.; *Medium:* Watercolor

FIGURE 4.8 **Elevation for a small library, c. 1930s.**
Design and illustration: Grace Fakes for McMillen Inc.; *Medium:* Watercolor

FIGURE 4.9 **Elevation for a small library, c. 1930s.**
Design and illustration: Grace Fakes for McMillen Inc.; *Medium:* Watercolor

David Payne (1907–1985) was a leading room painter for over 50 years, portraying the habitations of the wealthy society of New York and Newport. His individual style was interpreted using watercolors and occasionally oils and pastels. Payne's hand always seemed free, and his lines flowing. He captured detail and color while maintaining a looseness of technique.

"Payne tells us how this world he painted should be seen to best effect. He understood the look of sunlight on brocade and old wood, and of flowers in a room. His works are gracious little records of intimate intention, with which Payne himself seems utterly attuned. As a result, he opens up a particular, private world in a way no other form of record-keeping can." (Guralnick, Margot. 1989. The art of the interior. HG, February, page 201.)

FIGURE 4.10 **Living room, New York City, 1938.**
Artist: David Payne; *Medium:* Watercolor
(House & Garden's Complete Guide to Interior Decoration, *courtesy of House & Garden, Copyright © 1947 [renewed 1975] by The Condè Nast Publications Inc.*)

This very atmospheric, tonal perspective emphasizes the airiness and softness that the designers intended for the room. Rounded corners abound, from the shape of the fireplace frame to the deeply tufted footstool. A masking technique, employing crayon or chalk over a straight edge, may have created the outside edge of the rug and the ceiling line. (*Library of the Universtädt von Bilding Künst, Vienna.*)

FIGURE 4.11   **Living room, Vienna, 1936.**
Design and illustration: Professor Otto Preutscher, A. Schwerk, A. Roben; *Medium*: Blue pencil or graphite on trace

Walter Gay (1856–1937) moved from Massachusetts to Paris in 1876 and lived in France for the rest of his highly successful career, gaining fame as a world-renowned artist specializing in room paintings. He was a frequent exhibitor at the French salons, and his work is represented today in many museums and in private collections. Novelist Edith Wharton was one of his closest friends.

"There are no figures in these interpretations. The artist commemorates insensate things. Yet he fills his rooms with joy of living. They vibrate delicately with a friendly, gracious atmosphere." (1921. *Connoisseur*, January, page 190.)

FIGURE 4.12   **"The White Salon at Saint Brice," residence of Edith Wharton, Pavillon Colombe, France, 1931.**
Artist: Walter Gay; *Medium*: Oil on canvas
(1931. *International Studio, Vol. 99, May-August: frontispiece. Frick Art Reference Library, New York City.*)

Pencil shadings convey subtle textures and surfaces in these concept drawings for mass distribution furniture, lighting, and a floor-model radio.

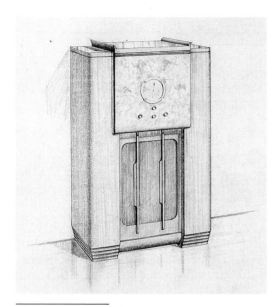

FIGURE 4.13   **Radio design, 1935. Console model #427.**

Design and illustration: L. Morgan Yost; *Medium:* Graphite on tracing paper

(*Gift of Mrs. L. Morgan Yost, 1990. Photo:* ©1993, *The Art Institute of Chicago. All Rights Reserved.*)

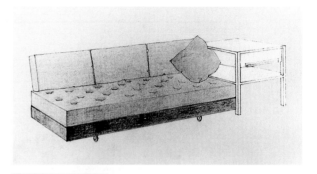

FIGURE 4.14   **Daybed design, c. 1930–1935.**

Design and illustration: Paul Schweikher; *Medium:* Colored pencil on line print

(*Gift of Dorothy and Paul Schweikher, 1984.801.9. Photo:* ©1993, *The Art Institute of Chicago. All Rights Reserved.*)

FIGURE 4.16   **Design and illustration by L. Morgan Yost for an upholstered chair, 1935.**

Medium: Graphite on tracing paper

(*Gift of L. Morgan Yost. Photo:* ©1993, *The Art Institute of Chicago. All Rights Reserved.*)

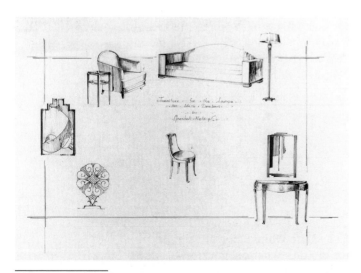

FIGURE 4.15   **Furniture proposal for the lounge of 1100 North Dearborn Street apartment building, Chicago, Illinois, c. 1930.**

Design and illustration: McNally and Quinn for Marshall Field and Company; *Medium:* Graphite on drawing board

(*Gift of J. Edwin Quinn, 1991.276.2. Photo:* ©1993, *The Art Institute of Chicago. All Rights Reserved.*)

FIGURE 4.17   **Living room chair or dining armchair, cherry with rattan seat, c. 1930–1935.**

Design and illustration: Paul Schweikher; *Medium:* Colored pencil on line print

(*Gift of Dorothy and Paul Schweikher. Photo:* ©1993, *The Art Institute of Chicago. All Rights Reserved.*)

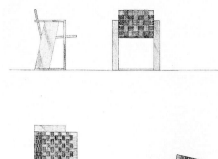

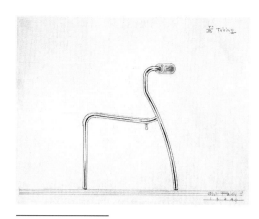

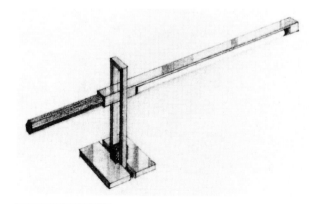

FIGURE 4.18   **Armchair with webbing, study for Chicago Workshop, c. 1930–1935.**
Design and illustration: Paul Schweikher; *Media:* Graphite and colored pencil on buff paper
(Gift of Dorothy and Paul Schweikher. Photo: ©1993, The Art Institute of Chicago. All Rights Reserved.)

FIGURE 4.19   **Side elevation of a tubular steel side chair, 1934.**
Design and illustration: Abel Faidy; *Medium:* Black and blue pencil on two-hole punched notepaper
(Gift of Diana Faidy, 1988.407.1. Photo: ©1993, The Art Institute of Chicago. All Rights Reserved.)

FIGURE 4.20   **Study for combined dining and study table, cherry and maple, c. 1930–1935.**
Design and illustration: Paul Schweikher; *Medium:* Colored pencil on line print
(Gift of Dorothy and Paul Schweikher. Photo: ©1993, The Art Institute of Chicago. All Rights Reserved.)

FIGURE 4.22   **Walnut floor lamp, c. 1930–1935.**
Design and illustration: Paul Schweikher; *Medium:* Colored pencil on line print
(Gift of Dorothy and Paul Schweikher. Photo: ©1993, The Art Institute of Chicago. All Rights Reserved.)

FIGURE 4.21   **Study lamp, birch and gum, c. 1930–1935.**
Design and illustration: Paul Schweikher; *Medium:* Colored pencil on line print
(Gift of Dorothy and Paul Schweikher. Photo: ©1993, The Art Institute of Chicago. All Rights Reserved.)

French architect Robert Mallet-Stevens was one of the founders in 1929 of the Union des Artistes Modernes, which welcomed new industrial materials and modern movement ideas. His visionary drawing for a modern schoolroom would suspend rows of chairs and desks from five metal girderlike supports. For

FIGURE 4.23   **Design for a classroom, 1936.**
Design and illustration: Robert Mallet-Stevens;
Medium: Pastel polychrome mounted on pressed paper
(*Musée des Arts Décoratifs, Paris. Photo: L. Sully-Jaulmes. Used with permission.*)

this high-contrast drawing, he incorporated the gradation of light from the full-height sliding glass doors to the deep shadows cast by the desk/seat units. The glistening reflective floor and desktop surfaces and dark shadows are vivid embellishments.

Figures 4.24 and 4.25 are interiors for Norwegian America Lines' *Oslofjord*, 1938.

Strong contrasts and highlights give drama to the renderings. From the magazine's descriptive caption: "The interior designer has combined the work of Norway's leading artists and craftsmen so that each room has acquired an individuality quite unusual in steamships. In the Leif Erikson Hall, the painting illustrates the discovery of America by Erikson. The dining salon has wide windows and gay colors." (1938. Interior design in transportation. *Interior Design and Decoration*, June, pages 34–35.)

FIGURE 4.24   **Leif Erikson Hall.**
(Designer unknown); *Illustrator*: M. Shion; *Medium*: Probably opaque paint

FIGURE 4.25   **Dining salon.**
(Designer unknown); *Illustrator*: M. Shion; *Medium*: Probably opaque paint

Cutaway views are used to see into otherwise very small spaces. (*a*) "A deluxe suite which includes private shower bath as well as movable lounge chairs and efficient lighting; (*b*) one end of the dining salon where bright flowers add to its intimate charm; (*c*) one end of the lounge car." (1938. Interior design in transportation. *Interior Design and Decoration*, June, page 30.)

FIGURE 4.26 Interiors for The New York Central's New Century train, 1938. Deluxe suite with movable lounge chairs and shower (*top*); dining salon with alcoves for fresh flowers (*center*); lounge car (*bottom*).

Design and illustration: Henry Dreyfuss; *Media*: Mixed

Figures 4.27 and 4.28 are maquette and detail drawings for commercial projects in New York City, 1930s.

FIGURE 4.27   **Lobby of a Fifth Avenue apartment building, 1938.**

Design and illustration: Grace Fakes for McMillen Incorporated; *Medium*: Watercolor

FIGURE 4.28   **Restaurant in a private club, 1934.**

Design and illustration: Grace Fakes for McMillen Incorporated; *Medium*: Watercolor

Stanley Barrows was affiliated with the Paris program run during the summer months by the New York School of Fine Art (later known as the Parsons School of Design) in the years between the world wars. His intimate, whimsical view in pen-and-ink and wash of a sweater display shows the economical use of space.

FIGURE 4.29   **Concept sketch for a retail apparel store, Paris, 1939.**

Design and illustration: Stanley Barrows; *Medium*: Watercolor

Mies van der Rohe, one of the original masters of the Bauhaus in Germany in the 1920s, emigrated to the United States in 1938 to head the architecture program at the University of Illinois. One of the icons of twentieth-century architecture, his design for the Barcelona chair and footstool (Figs. 3.24 and 3.25) has endured as one of the classics of modern furniture.

Sparse, quick strokes of ink on paper convey the large scope and elegant framework of the architect's design. (*Gift of A. James Speyer, 1981.936-937. Photo: ©1993, The Art Institute of Chicago. All Rights Reserved.*)

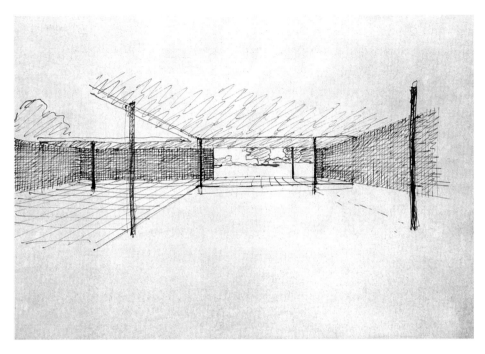

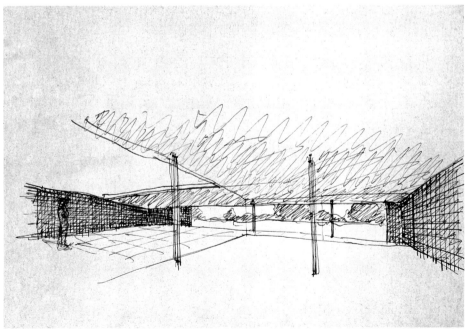

FIGURE 4.30   **Perspective studies for the interior of a courthouse with steel columns, c. 1931–1938.**

Design and illustration: Ludwig Mies van der Rohe; *Medium*: Pen-and-ink on paper

Fantasy rooms give the designer and renderer an opportunity to imagine unlimited budgets, no time constraints, or the restrictions of an existing floor plan. They bring pure creative energies to bear on the idea and can be inspiration for more realistic projects later on.

This fantasy room creates a jewel-like fantasy atmosphere utilizing two colors. The walls and ceiling are textured fabric, highlighted with decorative motifs. Wall-mounted tray tables hold jars and bottles. The low molded chaise seems to float. (*Library of the Universtädt von Bilding Künst, Vienna.*)

FIGURE 4.31   **One-point perspective study for a room in a spa, 1932.** (Designer and illustrator are unknown.) *Media*: Pen, ink, and tone wash

Throughout the 1930s, Hollywood headliners starring in musical spectacles and exotic action films gave moviegoers some respite from their Depression-era problems. Drawings by the film's art director would help the film's director visualize how a scene would register on camera from an ideal sight line. Figure 4.37 on the opposite page is an exception to this practice, where the steep angle down to the performers on stage was an imaginary stagehand's view from the rafters.

FIGURE 4.32   **Bridal suite for the RKO Studios film, *Top Hat*, starring Fred Astaire, 1935. (Mark Sandrich, director; Carroll Clark, art director.)** *Illustrator*: Allan Abbott; *Media*: Pencil and charcoal on board

(*Courtesy of the Museum of Modern Art, New York City.*)

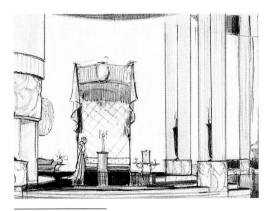

FIGURE 4.33 *Varsity Show,* Warner Bros., 1937, starring Dick Powell and Priscilla Lane, with Fred Waring and His Pennsylvanians. (Busby Berkeley and William Keighley, directors; music by Richard Whiting and Johnny Mercer.)

Illustrator and art director: Carroll Clark

(Margaret Herrick Library, Leo "K" Kuter Collection, Academy Foundation, Beverly Hills, California. Courtesy of Kay E. Kuter.)

FIGURE 4.34 Courtyard, *Captain Blood,* Warner Bros., 1935, starring Errol Flynn, Olivia de Havilland, and Basil Rathbone. (Michael Curtiz, director; Leo "K" Kuter, associate art director.)

Illustrator and art director: Anton Grot; *Medium:* Charcoal

(Margaret Herrick Library, Leo "K" Kuter Collection, Academy Foundation, Beverly Hills, California. Courtesy of Kay E. Kuter.)

FIGURE 4.35 Interior of Maximilian's headquarters at Convent La Cruz, *Juarez,* Warner Bros., 1939, starring Bette Davis, Brian Ahern, Paul Muni, and Claude Rains. (William Dieterle, director.)

Illustrator and art director: Leo "K" Kuter; *Medium:* Charcoal

(Margaret Herrick Library, Leo "K" Kuter Collection, Academy Foundation, Beverly Hills, California. Courtesy of Kay E. Kuter.)

FIGURE 4.36 Performance of The Dancing Dolans, *On Your Toes,* Warner Bros., 1939, starring Vera Zorina, Eddie Albert, and Donald O'Connor. (Ray Enright, director; Anton Grot, art director.)

Medium: Charcoal

(Margaret Herrick Library, Leo "K" Kuter Collection, Academy Foundation, Beverly Hills, California. Courtesy of Kay E. Kuter.)

FIGURE 4.37 Believed to be "Le Petit Harlem" dance sequence, *Fools for Scandal,* Warner Bros., 1937, starring Carole Lombard, Ralph Bellamy, and Fernand Gravet. (Mervyn LeRoy, director and producer, songs by Richard Rodgers and Lorenz Hart; Anton Grot, art director.)

Illustrator and associate art director: Attributed to Leo "K" Kuter; *Medium:* Charcoal

(Margaret Herrick Library, Leo "K" Kuter Collection, Academy Foundation, Beverly Hills, California. Courtesy of Kay E. Kuter.)

CHAPTER FIVE

1940 *to* 1949

During the World War II years, the theme was a patriotic "make-do-and-mend." In England, clothing and household goods were manufactured under a rigorous set of standards known as *Utility*. Then, in 1947, two years after the end of the war, French couturier Christian Dior's extravagant "New Look" in women's fashion signaled the end of wartime austerity. Interior design projects halted by the war revived concurrently with apparel, and traditional, period, and modern furnishing styles all flourished simultaneously.

Synthetic materials that were created by wartime conditions—plastics, polymers, nylon, and additional inventions for fabrics and other functional products—were now utilized by designers. The "Eclectic Look" found its way into the popular lexicon to describe traditional and antique furniture and accessories that were mixed with contemporary styles.

New York's Museum of Modern Art (MOMA) led the crusade to educate the American public about modern design, mounting in 1940 the "Organic Design in Home Furnishings" show. The postwar exhibition, "Modern Rooms of the Last 50 Years," traced the modern interior from William Morris to 1947, when the show opened. In 1949, MOMA's first "Good Design" show included the products of such postwar master architect-designers as Alexander Girard and Russel Wright. Products in MOMA's permanent collection are judged for their excellence in form, material, craftsmanship, and function.

Furniture created by designers trained at the Cranbrook Academy in Bloomfield Hills, Michigan, first appeared in the 1940s. Charles and Ray Eames, Eero Saarinen, and Harry Bertoia brought "good design to the masses."

The first mass-produced plastic seating was Charles Eames' shell chair. Its single-molded, ergonomically designed seat and back made of fiberglass reinforced polyester resin made it light, durable, and easy to store.

Two leading American manufacturers, Knoll Furniture Company and Herman Miller, rose to prominence in this decade. Florence and Hans Knoll established the Knoll Planning Unit for interior design in 1946, concentrating primarily on contract (nonresidential) interiors. The firm's classic furniture line was based on geometrically inspired silhouettes and expensive finishes. In 1946, Herman Miller began to mass-produce examples of modern furniture created by such sculptors as Isamu Noguchi whose palette-shaped glass-topped table became a standard of the period. George Nelson's 1949 "Basic Storage Components" for Herman Miller which consisted of open shelving, drawers, a cupboard and desk, and a nonsupporting wall/space divider became a whole new furniture category. Herman Miller's output is now concentrated on systems furniture for offices, health care, and manufacturing uses.

In 1946, the now-international furniture retailing chain, IKEA, was founded in Sweden, which remained neutral during the war. IKEA's modern, attractively priced furnishings for the home (and now home offices) are now found in stores in Europe, the Far East, and since 1987, in the United States.

Magazines carried the story of American design. *Domus* brought it to Italy where the Italian manufacturing firm, Cassina, produced designs by editor Gio Ponti, Vico Magistratti, and Mario Bellini. Running parallel to the contemporary mood in design was a revival of traditionalism and eclecticism, a "bring back romance" movement that was a welcome relief form the war years.

Firms such as Dorothy Draper & Company developed an interior design specialty for hotels and large commercial projects. Ms. Draper, the older sister of interior designer Mrs. Henry Parish III, had started her own business in 1925. Her style evolved into pure high drama, combining crisp classicism with huge scale and bold colors; the Greenbrier Hotel in West Virginia, the Fairmount Hotel in San Francisco, and the Metropolitan Museum of Art restaurant were some of her firm's most visible public projects.

A return to a peacetime economy meant more disposable income for consumers to spend on new products for the home, promoted in shelter magazines by major retailers and manufacturers.

The movie industry provided entertainment during the war years for the home front and the troops overseas. Sets for such classic films as *Dispatch from Reuters* and *Now, Voyager* were created by pioneer art directors Anton Grot, Leo "K" Kuter, and Robert Haas whose careers continued well into the postwar period. Mr. Kuter collected and organized hundreds of his drawings and those of his colleagues along with photographs of the sets to form one of the most extensive collections of sketches and photos of the period from the 1920s to the 1960s, a period often referred to as the "Golden Age of Hollywood." The collection is now in the archives of the Margaret Herrick Library at the Academy of Motion Picture Arts and Sciences in Beverly Hills, California.

Hugh Ferriss, Master Illustrator
(See Fig. 5.20, ground level of the Administration Building,
S. C. Johnson Wax Company, Racine, Wisconsin, 1941.)

Without question, Hugh Ferriss (1889–1962) was this nation's most celebrated and influential architectural illustrator. Born in St. Louis and trained as an architect, Ferriss elected to draw rather than build. Ferriss defined the art of rendering as "an attempt to tell the truth about a building." Truth was more than simple reporting of structural facts. "Buildings possess an individual existence, varying—now dynamic, now serene—but vital, as all else in the universe." His visions . . . serve as more than inspiration to generations of architects and artists. They proved to be highly instrumental in shaping much of what was to become the best of [his era's] modern architecture.

(*Architecture in Perspective*. 1992. New York: Van Nostrand Reinhold, page 46.)

Albert Hadley used a light, quick, energetic felt-tip pen technique to depict this living room. One of the great masters of the interior design profession, Mr. Hadley's illustration style has remained virtually unchanged for over a half-century.

FIGURE 5.1 **Living room, New York City, 1941.**
Design: Parish-Hadley Associates Incorporated (Albert Hadley);
Illustrator: Albert Hadley, FASID; *Medium*: Felt-tip pen

Boston's Jordan Marsh department store publicized the opening of its Baker Furniture Gallery with a full-page advertisement in a national magazine. The illustration of the living room includes a mirrored wall that adds depth and style to the setting. (*House & Garden*, June 1948, page 1.)

FIGURE 5.2 **Advertisement for a living room, 1946.**
Illustrator: Max Walter; *Media*: Pen-and-ink and wash

Executed in the 1940s as part of the course in interior design at the Parsons School of Design, New York City, the room's styling was influenced by the Directoire period. (*Courtesy of Stanley Barrows.*)

FIGURE 5.3   Music room in the late-eighteenth-century Italian style.
Illustrator: M. K. Young; *Medium:* Watercolor

Albert Hadley trained with the legendary interior designer, Elsie de Wolfe, before starting his own business in the early 1960s with the late Mrs. Henry ("Sister") Parish III. His distinctive loose sketch technique is a viable tool to quickly communicate the ambience of a room he has designed.

FIGURE 5.4   Bedroom for a Hollywood, California, client of the interior design firm headed by Elsie de Wolfe, 1945.
Design and illustration: Albert Hadley, FASID;
Medium: Felt-tip pen

The caption written by the magazine's editors advises, "When you remodel a farmhouse, turn kitchen and parlor into one large room." José Méndez was a talented furniture designer as well as a skilled delineator. His work for the influential industrial design firm of Raymond Loewy/William Snaith is included in Chap. 6 (Figs. 6.11 to 6.13). (*House & Garden*, February 1948, page 92.)

FIGURE 5.5 **Living room and food preparation area.**
Illustrator: José M. Reinares Méndez;
Media: Watercolor and pen-and-ink

To promote the new Burlington House Hanover Satin lines of rayon and cotton decorative fabrics, this softly rendered setting shows upholstery fabric used on a pair of facing settees, on a pair of chairs (partial view, right), and as a floor-to-ceiling room divider that frames the dining area. (*House & Garden*, June 1948, page 144.)

FIGURE 5.6 **Advertisement illustration by Burlington Mills for fabrics for a living room and dining area.**
Illustrator: Max Warshow;
Medium: Watercolor

The firm's "Dream House" line of slipcovers was a promotional tie-in with the film, *Mr. Blandings Builds His Dream House*, which starred Cary Grant, Myrna Loy, and Melvyn Douglas. (*House & Garden*, June 1948, page 22.)

FIGURE 5.7   **Illustrations from full-page ad placed by Sure-Fit Products Company.**
Medium: Probably watercolor

Consumers found that slipcovers and draperies were a quick and inexpensive way to redecorate during the postwar recovery period. Chintz-like products such as Schumacher's Glosheen promised washability and long wear. The fanciful pink/green/black color scheme was softly rendered and vignetted in the foreground. (*House & Garden*, June 1948, page 33).

FIGURE 5.8   **Illustration from full-page ad placed by Waverly Fabrics Division, F. Schumacher & Company.**
Illustrator: Signed "Ian";
Medium: Watercolor

The refined lines of modern furniture began to appear more frequently in the transitional rooms created for residential and commercial applications by the decade's leading interior designers. Figures 5.9 to 5.13 are maquettes and custom furniture pieces commissioned for projects in the 1940s.

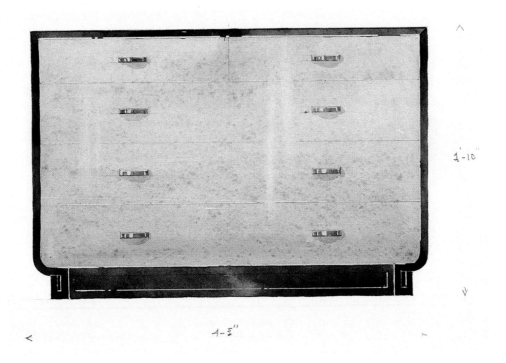

FIGURE 5.9   **Dresser.**
Design: McMillen Inc.; *Illustrator*: Grace Fakes; *Medium*: Watercolor

FIGURE 5.10   **Wall elevation of a New York City dining room.**
Design: McMillen Inc.; *Illustrator*: Grace Fakes; *Medium*: Watercolor

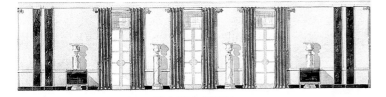

FIGURE 5.11   Elevations of walls in a lobby of River House, New York City.
Design: McMillen Inc.; *Illustrator*: Grace Fakes; *Medium*: Watercolor

FIGURE 5.12   Maquette of a card room in a private club.
Design: McMillen Inc.; *Illustrator*: Grace Fakes; *Medium*: Watercolor

FIGURE 5.13   Wall elevation of an entry hall.
Design: McMillen Inc.; *Illustrator*: Grace Fakes; *Medium*: Watercolor

"Reminiscent of a musicale in a French salon . . . Steinway's Sheraton grand, in mahogany with exquisite inlay . . . around it are five identical black-and-white Regency chairs. The curtain design is from an old French engraving." Shown: all furniture, Baker; wallpaper, Strahan's Regency medallion. (*House & Garden*, January, 1940, page 31.)

FIGURE 5.14 **Music room.**
Illustrator: Credited to Weis; *Medium*: Watercolor

Ernest Walker's drawing looks as fresh and stylish today as it did when it first appeared over a half-century ago. (*House & Garden*, December 1943, page 73.)

FIGURE 5.15 **Caribbean-style bedroom.**
Illustrator: Ernest Walker; *Medium*: Watercolor

Advertisements of sleek postwar kitchens and dining areas stimulated demand as factory output shifted from wartime products to consumer goods. The dinette set ad also carried the endorsement of film star Esther Williams, along with her photo. Today, ads for "dinettes" are rare. The Frigidaire kitchen was state of the art in 1948: an electric range with an optional double oven, timer, and other labor-saving features and benefits.

FIGURE 5.16   **Illustration from full-page ad placed by the Chromcraft Division of the American Fixture & Manufacturing Company.**
Illustrator: Biondi; *Media*: Possibly watercolor and airbrush
(*House & Garden*, June 1948, page 34.)

FIGURE 5.17   **Illustration from a full-page ad placed by General Motors' Frigidaire division.**
Illustrator: Albert Dorne; *Media*: Possibly watercolor and airbrush
(*House & Garden*, June 1948, page 35.)

Figure 5.18 shows a variety of postwar consumer products for the home. Drawings and quotes from *Good Design Is Your Business*, 1947, ©The Buffalo Fine Arts Academy, Albright Art Gallery, Buffalo, New York. *(Courtesy of Elizabeth Porter, AIA.)*

FIGURE 5.18*a*   *Lawn barrow.* Dow Engineers for Specialty Products Division, The Dow Chemical Company. "... a rhythmic combination of lines and forms eminently right for light gardening."

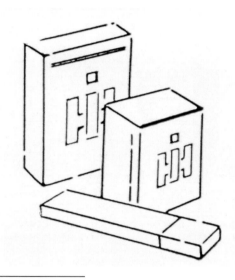

FIGURE 5.18*b*   *Tools and parts packages.* Raymond Loewy Associates for International Harvester Company. "The sturdy lettering in red and black, bold against the natural paperboard or gray background ... symbolic of the garage and shop ..."

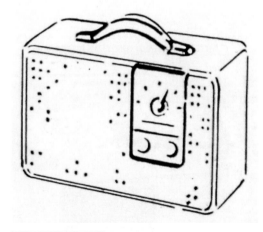

FIGURE 5.18*c*   *Portable radio.* Raymond Loewy Associates for Emerson Radio and Phonograph Corporation. "Mr. Loewy has made the most of the three components offered him—control panel, cabinet, and sound outlet—playing one visual texture against another."

FIGURE 5.18*d*   *Electric flat iron.* Francesco Collura and John Polivka for General Mills, "... a departure from traditional design ... the designers achieve a clean form of beautiful proportions."

FIGURE 5.18f *Cooking utensil.* Revere Copper and Brass. "Black plastic handles accentuate the gleaming metal and call attention to the gently curving surfaces."

FIGURE 5.18e *Electric kitchen mixer.* Egmont Arens for Kitchen Aid Division, The Hobart Manufacturing Company. "Few mixers can equal this in appropriateness of line or suitability of mass; [it is a product] of cooperative effort of designer and engineer."

FIGURE 5.18g *Bowl and vase.* Alexander Giampietro for Cunningham Potters. Free-form molded stoneware.

FIGURE 5.18h *Low wood chair.* Charles Eames for Evans Products Company, Molded Plywood Division. "The success with which lightness and elegance have been combined with strength enhances this articulation."

FIGURE 5.18i *Electric fan.* Samson United Corporation. "Implicit in this design are the flow of air and versatility of adjustment on wall or table."

Dorothy Draper (1889–1969) founded her own firm in 1925, and specialized in hotels, restaurants, clubs, lobbies, and other commercial projects. Her associate, Carleton Varney, now heads the firm. (*Courtesy of Albert Hadley*, FASID.)

FIGURE 5.19   **Design for a hotel lobby, 1946.**
Design: Dorothy Draper & Company; *Illustrator*: John Marsman; *Medium*: Felt-tip pen

Illustrator Hugh Ferriss, who was trained as an architect, helped to elevate architectural rendering to the status of a profession. (One of his major early drawings is Fig. 2.22, the banking area of the Woolworth Building.) This drawing of the main workroom does not show the desks and chairs that Wright designed for the workers, but rather shows the unoccupied space at eye level, focusing the viewer on the monumentality of the concrete column system. Ferris implies almost a futuristic view, with the receding architectural forms becoming increasingly lighter in shading, and the outlines of small human forms barely discernable in the far background.

The slender, tapered concrete columns are flared and corrugated at the top. Wright's layout for the main workroom was an early "open office" concept, but without sound absorbing workspace dividers, which were to be introduced nearly 25 years after completion of the Johnson project. (*The Hugh Ferriss Collection, Avery Library, Columbia University, New York City.*)

FIGURE 5.20   Administration Building, S. C. Johnson Wax Company, Racine, Wisconsin. (This drawing was produced c. 1941; the building was completed in 1939.)
Design: Frank Lloyd Wright; *Illustrator*: Hugh Ferriss; *Media*: Pencil and charcoal on paper on board

The designer chose a hard-edged black and white linear technique to produce a visually dramatic presentation for a private club. (*Courtesy of Cooper-Hewitt Museum, New York City.*)

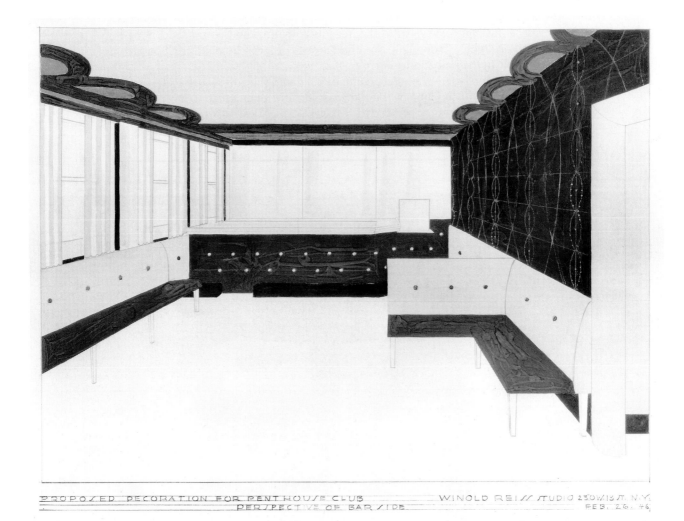

FIGURE 5.21   **Proposed design for the bar area of the Penthouse Club, 1946.**
Design and illustration: Winold Reiss; *Medium*: Pen-and-ink and pencil

For figures 5.22 through 5.29 (this page and next two pages), a well-composed drawing can condense the mood of a dramatic scene in a manner that a photo of the same setting cannot approach. The visual depiction of film sets, which is a distinct genre of interior rendering, previews what the movie camera will capture and the emotions that audiences will experience. Shown on these three pages are drawings that were constructed into sets for famous films of the 1940s. They effectively unite the spaces with the actors and the script.

FIGURE 5.22 *Citizen Kane*, RKO Pictures, 1941. (Orson Welles, director; Perry Ferguson, art director.)
Illustrator: Claude Gillingwater; *Media*: Pencil and charcoal on paper mounted on board
(*Courtesy of the Museum of Modern Art, New York City.*)

FIGURE 5.23   Corridor in a courthouse, from
The Gay Sisters, Warner Brothers, 1942, starring
Barbara Stanwyck, Geraldine Fitzgerald, and
George Brent. (Irving Rapper, director.)

Illustrator: Attributed to Harper Goff

*(Margaret Herrick Library, Leo "K" Kuter Collection, Academy
Foundation, Beverly Hills, California. Courtesy of Kay E. Kuter.)*

FIGURE 5.24   Grand salon in an oceanliner, from
'Til We Meet Again, Warner Brothers, 1940, starring
Merle Oberon, Pat O'Brien, and George Brent.
(Edmund Goulding, director.)

Illustrator: Attributed to Fritz Willis or Harold Cox III

*(Margaret Herrick Library, Leo "K" Kuter Collection, Academy
Foundation, Beverly Hills, California. Courtesy of Kay E. Kuter.)*

FIGURE 5.25   Restaurant scene in *To Have and To
Have Not*, Warner Brothers, 1945, starring Lauren
Bacall, Humphrey Bogart, and Walter Brennan.
(Howard Hawks, director; Charles Novi, art
director.)

Illustrator: Attributed to Travis Johnson

*(Margaret Herrick Library, Leo "K" Kuter Collection, Academy
Foundation, Beverly Hills, California. Courtesy of Kay E. Kuter.)*

FIGURE 5.26   Barroom scene in *Flamingo Road*,
Warner Brothers, 1949, starring Joan Crawford and
Sidney Greenstreet. (Michael Curtiz, director; Leo
"K" Kuter, art director.)

Illustrator: Attributed to Tyrus Wong

*(Margaret Herrick Library, Leo "K" Kuter Collection, Academy
Foundation, Beverly Hills, California. Courtesy of Kay E. Kuter.)*

FIGURE 5.27   The main hall at Fitzroy in the movie
In This Our Life, Warner Brothers, 1942, starring
Bette Davis, Charles Coburn, Dennis Morgan, and
George Brent. (John Houston, director; Robert
Haas, art director.)

Illustrator: Attributed to Harper Goff

*(Margaret Herrick Library, Leo "K" Kuter Collection, Academy
Foundation, Beverly Hills, California. Courtesy of Kay E. Kuter.)*

FIGURE 5.29   Lower hall of the Wheelwright home
from *Million Dollar Baby*, Warner Brothers, 1941,
starring Priscilla Lane and Ronald Reagan. (Curtis
Bernhardt, director.)

*(Margaret Herrick Library, Leo "K" Kuter Collection, Academy
Foundation, Beverly Hills, California. Courtesy of Kay E. Kuter.)*

FIGURE 5.28   Hall of the Vale home from *Now,
Voyager*, Warner Brothers, 1942, starring Bette
Davis, Claude Rains, Paul Henreid, and Ilka Chase.
(Irving Rapper, director; Robert Haas, art director;
Leo "K" Kuter, associate art director.)

Illustrator: Attributed to Harper Goff

*(Margaret Herrick Library, Leo "K" Kuter Collection, Academy
Foundation, Beverly Hills, California. Courtesy of Kay E. Kuter.)*

FIGURE 5.30   Courtyard of the London Stock
Exchange, from *Dispatch from Reuters*, Warner
Brothers, 1942, starring Edward G. Robinson, Edna
Best, and Eddie Albert. (William Dieterle,
director; Anton Grot, art director; Leo "K" Kuter,
associate art director.)

Illustrator: Leo "K" Kuter

*(Margaret Herrick Library, Leo "K" Kuter Collection, Academy
Foundation, Beverly Hills, California. Courtesy of Kay E. Kuter.)*

CHAPTER SIX

1950
to
1959

Modern design gained recognition as the framework for highly original and thoughtful interiors. Milan emerged as a creative force in the contemporary furniture industry with furniture and accessories that were fresh and appealing. *Scandinavian modern* began to hit its stride as a mainstay of popular residential interiors. *Design in Sweden* toured U.S. and Canadian cities between 1954 and 1957 to wide acclaim. Swedish system and modular furniture was quickly appreciated and adapted to the taste of young postwar couples furnishing their first home. The functional forms and basic wood and steel construction made the style well-suited for offices and other "contract" or commercial projects. *It's Danish* was verbal shorthand to describe the decade's new look.

Fiberglass, once used primarily as a material for molding boat hulls and fittings, turned into the furniture product of the decade. Architect Eero Saarinen's molded fiberglass pedestal chair, with and without arms, was adapted for both home and commercial uses. In 1950, the Planner Group, designed by Paul McCobb, was a popular-priced line introduced in department and furniture specialty stores. One of the first mass-produced residential modular groupings, it used traditional birch and maple in simple constructions.

Glass and aluminum were prominently used in everything from building skins to kitchen furniture. Textile design—intricate patterns, textures, and striking color combinations—lent personality and individualism to contemporary rooms and public spaces. Weaver and textile designer Jack Lenoir Larsen opened his own studio in 1952. The firm has grown in size and continues to offer a broad line of fabrics and accessories.

The electronic age planted itself firmly in homes and apartments. Television and sound-reproduction equipment entered living rooms, dens, and other living areas. Modular furniture was particularly suited to organizing a family entertainment center. With horizontal surfaces that could be adjusted for height, and whole units for storage and shelving that could be purchased as required, flexibility quickly caught on as an accepted furnishings concept.

Consumers could, of course, still exercise their traditional taste preferences with reproductions of furniture of previous eras now repackaged as French Provincial, Italian Provincial, and Early American. Shipments of antique furniture and accessories from Europe and the Orient, halted for nearly two decades because of wartime conditions, began to arrive in the United States and attracted a whole new generation of buyers.

The modern kitchen now offered equipment that was anchored to the wall rather than free-standing had evolved since the early 1930s when manufacturers began to redesign their kitchen equipment lines to boost lagging sales that came with the Depression. Two major American consumer appliance manufacturers, General Electric and Westinghouse, had opened cooking institutes to investigate how to improve kitchen design. As a result of suggestions from cooks, engineers, and architects, the institutes came up with a new room arrangement in which stove, sink, refrigerator, and cabinets were placed flat against the walls in configurations most efficient for the cook.

The next important advance came in 1946 when Thermador announced a stove designed, not as separate unit, but as part of the architecture of the kitchen. Thermador's built-in oven went directly into the wall, while the range unit, with burners set into a sheet of stainless steel, plugged into the countertop. In the mid-1950s, manufacturers such as General Electric and Kitchen Maid put the finishing touch on the trend toward built-ins with a kitchen in which stove, refrigerator, and sink were all part of the room's architecture.

Tract houses in the suburbs were designed with eat-in kitchens large enough to accommodate a new category of furniture, the dinette set. Unlike earlier versions of the kitchen table, which were of wood or combined wood with metal or a composite material, dinettes were nearly always fabricated of metal and plastic; chairs were typically covered in vinyl.

Walter Gropius, who was the first director of the Bauhaus in Germany in 1919 that sought to bridge the gap between between art and industry, ultimately emigrated to the United States where in 1949 he helped to found The Architects Collaborative in Cambridge, Massachusetts. Frank Lloyd Wright was working in a much more organic and sculptural way in the postwar era. For the Solomon R. Guggenheim Museum (1959) on Fifth Avenue in New York, a single internal spiral ramp comprises the main exhibition space. In 1957, architect Louis I. Kahn, one of the most revered of American architects and design theorists, became a professor of architecture at the University of Pennsylvania, a post he held until his death in 1974. His powerfully formed buildings include the Kimbell Art Museum in Fort Worth, Texas, and the Salk Institute Laboratories in La Jolla, California.

Curtain wall construction was established as the construction technique of choice for skyscrapers for coming decades. Three New York City structures gave evidence of this fact: Lever House (1950–1952) by Skidmore, Owings & Merrill; the United Nations Building (1951–1952) by Wallace K. Harrison and Associates; and the Seagram Building (1956–1958) by Mies van der Rohe. Philip Johnson opened his own office in 1954. Johnson's elegant, imaginative design for the Four Seasons restaurant, on the Seagram Building's ground floor, maintains its freshness and originality today, nearly 40 years later.

Le Corbusier was the dominant figure in French postwar architectural design. With the Nôtre-Dame-du-Haute chapel at Ronchamp, Haute-Saône

(1950–1954), he created a dynamic space that features a hanging ceiling. The parabolic shape of the building is highly sculptural in comparison with the clean geometric lines of his prewar work. Inside the chapel, the thick concrete walls are pierced by small stained glass windows designed by Le Corbusier to create the dramatic effect of shafts of colored light falling on the congregation (Fig. 6-21).

> "Client and interior designer agreed on a conservative modern scheme, with custom-designed pieces to fill the unique requirements of a busy woman executive in New York City . . . The simple, quiet appearance of the two-room apartment serves its purpose . . . as an informal gathering place for groups of out-of-town retail store buyers." (Adapted from the descriptive text, *Interior Design and Decoration*, August 1950, Vol. 28, No. 8.)

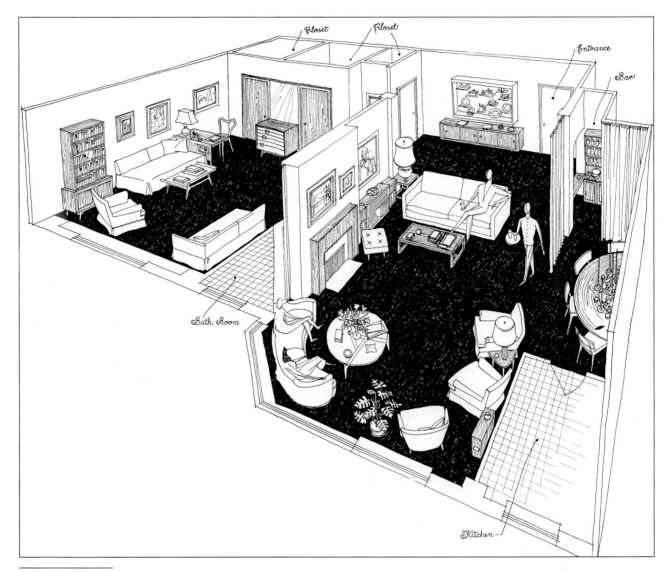

FIGURE 6.1   Bird's-eye view floor plan of a small urban apartment.
Design: Mrs. O. H. Garrison; *Illustrator*: Jorgen Gronberg Hansen; *Medium*: Pen-and-ink

The loose watercolor technique evokes the eclectic environment in a living area in one of the last private mansions in midtown before it was demolished. Fortunately, foundations have saved the former New York City homes on upper Fifth Avenue of Andrew Carnegie (now the Cooper-Hewitt Museum), Henry Clay Frick, and the Jay P. Morgan mansion on Madison Avenue, all now museums. (*Courtesy of Albert Hadley, FASID.*)

FIGURE 6.2 **Sitting room in the Vanderbilt Mansion (demolished), Fifth Avenue, New York City, c. 1950s.**
Illustrator: Student project, Parsons School of Design; *Medium*: Watercolor

Figures 6.3 and 6.4 are examples of a delicate technique of rendering elevations, favored by leading design schools.

FIGURE 6.3   **Two-story-high drawing room, New York City, c. 1951.**
Illustrator: Third-year student illustration project, Parsons School of Design;
Medium: Pen-and-ink, color marker

(*Courtesy of Stanley Barrows.*)

FIGURE 6.4   **Dining room in an Italian palazzo, c. 1950s.**
Illustrator: J. Hyde Crawford; *Medium*: Watercolor

Maquettes form a bridge between conceptual architectural drawing and decorative presentation. The architect visualizes the space as a floor plan and elevation; the artist then renders the floor plan and elevation to make it appear three-dimensional.

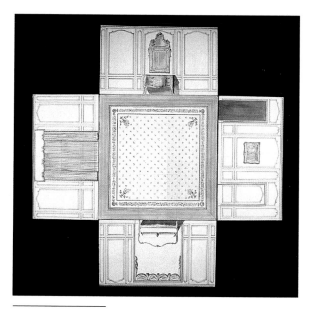

FIGURE 6.6   Maquette for living room design, c. 1950s. *Design*: McMillen Inc.; *Illustrator*: Grace Fakes; *Medium*: Watercolor

FIGURE 6.5   **Maquette of a bedroom, New York City, 1958.**
Design and illustration: Ernest L. Brothers; *Medium*: Watercolor
(*National Building Museum, Washington, D.C. Photo by Mark Strassman.*)

A black-and-white color scheme and clean, crisp watercolor washes accentuate the elegance of this period room. (*Courtesy of Stanley Barrows.*)

FIGURE 6.7   **French Empire-style dining room;** drawing executed in 1952 by an interior design student at the Parsons School of Design, New York City.

The viewer has the opportunity to view this space through a cutaway ceiling in an isometric done in a loose painterly style. Two walls and the floor form the background. (*Courtesy of Stanley Barrows.*)

FIGURE 6.8   Perspective drawing of a living room executed in the 1950s, part of the requirements of the interior design program at the Parsons School of Design, New York City.

Design and illustration: Leslie Land; *Media*: Watercolor with gouache

This student utilized two colors to communicate the intent of the design. (*Courtesy of Stanley Barrows.*)

FIGURE 6.9   A design student's version of a paneled drawing room, 1954, Parsons School of Design, New York City.

Medium: Watercolor

Joseph Martin defined his objects with tones of color and white background paper rather than with black outlines. The clear portrayal of the proposed colors for the room moves the eye around the drawing. (*House & Garden*, April 1952, page 44.)

FIGURE 6.10   **Living room, April, 1952.**

Illustrator: Joseph Martin; *Medium*: Watercolor

The spareness of the line technique complements the modern furniture styles developing in this decade. The industrial design firm of Raymond Loewy/ William Snaith was one of the multidisciplinary design innovators of the era. The original drawings were executed in pencil and pastel on vellum. Only black-and-white drawings currently exist. (*Courtesy of John W. Blackwell.*)

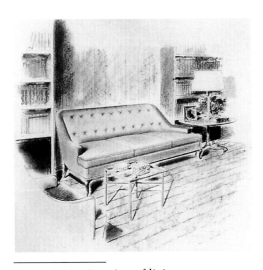

FIGURE 6.11 **Drawing of living room furniture designed in the 1950s.**

Design: Raymond Loewy/William Snaith Incorporated; *Illustrator*: José M. Reinares Méndez

FIGURE 6.12 **Drawing of living room furniture designed in the 1950s.**

Design: Raymond Loewy/William Snaith Incorporated; *Illustrator*: José M. Reinares Méndez

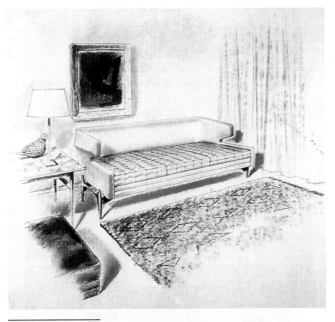

FIGURE 6.13 **Drawing of living room furniture designed in the 1950s.**

Design: Raymond Loewy/William Snaith Incorporated; *Illustrator*: José M. Reinares Méndez

FIGURE 6.14 Partial view of living area, looking toward the two-tier window treatment above plaid fabric-covered banquette.
Illustrator: Charles Heilemann; *Medium*: Watercolor

The dividing wall has been visually removed so the viewer can see into both adjacent spaces. On the floor in white is the outline of the actual wall in place and the furniture arrangement. (*Interior Design and Decoration*, August 1950, page 32.)

FIGURE 6.15 **Living room and library.**
Illustrator: Betty Freese; *Medium*: Watercolor

In the 1950s, furniture retailers began to promote a composed and coordinated look for rooms in new suburban homes and garden apartments. Matching slipcovers and draperies were an important stylistic trend. The decade witnessed the growth of advertising art to promote mass merchandising. Today, photography is the more popular illustrative medium employed by merchandisers to sell their products.

The department store chain, Lord & Taylor, which was for many years a home furnishings tastemaker, here showed a daybed and window covering in a matching plaid fabric. The loosely drawn cityscape view seen through the window is a pleasant urban touch. Lord & Taylor is now an apparel specialty store. (*House & Garden*, April 1952, page 115.)

FIGURE 6.16 **Illustration used in advertisement placed by Lord & Taylor.**
Illustrator: Arnold Hall; *Medium*: Watercolor

Syrie Maugham, wife of the writer Somerset Maugham, was a leading British society decorator for more than 25 years, starting in the 1930s. Her famous "all-white room" became a symbol of the acceptance of modern design for tasteful European interiors. This boudoir, or slipper chair, was distributed commercially in the United States. (*Interior Design & Decoration*, June 1950, page 71.)

FIGURE 6.17 **"The Dolphin Chair."**
Design: Syrie Maugham; *Medium*: Watercolor

The professional monthly journal, founded as *Interior Design and Decoration*, is a prestigious periodical read by architects and interiors specialists. For its cover in August 1950, illustrator John R. Hull created a delightful montage that captures the activities of the tradespeople and the items that go into a room's design.

FIGURE 6.18   Cover of *Interior Design and Decoration*, August 1950.
Illustrator: John R. Hull; *Media*: Mixed

To satisfy the pent-up consumer demand from the gray war years, and to sell the new modern lifestyle of the 1950s, manufacturers of mass-marketed dinette furniture turned to bright colors such as leaf green and chrome yellow. Fiestaware, now a collectible dinnerware, echoed these colors in pottery.

FIGURE 6.19   Illustration used in advertisement placed by Virtue Brothers Manufacturing Company. (*House & Garden*, March 1952, page 124.)
Medium: Watercolor

FIGURE 6.20   Advertisement placed by Kuehne Manufacturing Company. (*House & Garden*, April 1952, page 116.)
Medium: Watercolor

Architect Le Corbusier here used one-point perspective in a freehand manner to develop the design for the curvulinear interior of his famed Chapel at Ronchamp. This was one of Le Corbusier's most important works and is regarded as a masterpiece of modern architecture. He turned from the geometric forms of his earlier International Style to a more organic and sculptural design vocabulary. The interior has splashes of color from light filtering through stained glass windows of his design.

Le Corbusier's prolific output totaled over 450,000 drawings during his distinguished career. (*Fondation Le Corbusier, Paris.*)

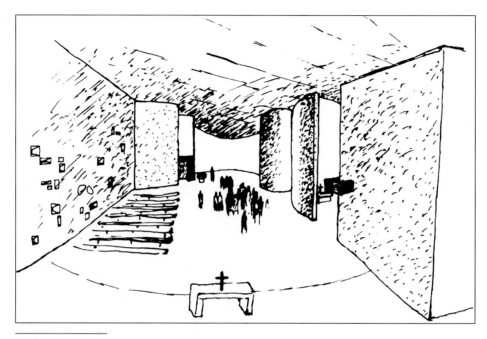

FIGURE 6.21   The Nôtre-Dame-du-Haute Chapel at Ronchamp, Haute-Saône, France, 1951.

Design and illustration: Le Corbusier; *Medium:* Pen-and-ink or pencil

The great architect Walter Gropius worked with others to execute his renderings and drawings. Here, the drama of the synagogue's interior is emphasized by the slashing lines of diagonal light radiating from the windows. The low horizon emphasizes the spiritual nature of the space and gives importance to its height. (Gropius, Walter, and Sarah P. Harkness. *The Architects Collaborative 1945–1965.* 1966. Teufen, Switzerland: Arthur Niggli, page 109.)

FIGURE 6.22   Interior view of Temple Oheb Shalom, Baltimore, Maryland, 1957.

Design: The Architects Collaborative, Walter Gropius, principal-in-charge; *Illustrator:* Jacek von Henneberg; *Medium:* Probably pencil

Silhouetted figures lead the eye from the foreground into the succession of spaces. The perspective gains visual quality by the different textures used to indicate trees, walls, and decorative surfaces. (*The Walter Gropius Archive—The Works of The Architects Collaborative*, pages 204 and 205. Courtesy of The Architects Collaborative and John C. Harkness, FAIA.)

FIGURE 6.23 **Balconied lobby and court, the University of Baghdad, Baghdad, Iraq, 1957.** *Design*: The Architects Collaborative, Walter Gropius and H. Morse Payne, principals-in-charge; *Illustrator*: H. Morse Payne; *Medium*: Pen-and-ink or felt-tip marker

FIGURE 6.24 **Balconied lobby and court, the University of Baghdad, Baghdad, Iraq, 1957.** *Design*: The Architects Collaborative, Walter Gropius and H. Morse Payne, principals-in-charge; *Illustrator*: H. Morse Payne; *Medium*: Pen-and-ink or felt-tip marker

Figures 6.25 and 6.26 are concept drawings executed in the 1950s. Pencil and pastel on vellum were used for the original drawings (only black-and-white prints currently exist).

The Loewy/Snaith office produced designs for manufacturers of consumer products, industrial components and housings, and interiors. (*Courtesy of John W. Blackwell.*)

FIGURE 6.25   **Lobby.**
Design: Raymond Loewy/William Snaith Incorporated; *Illustrator*: José M. Reinares Méndez

FIGURE 6.26   **Prototype design for Lord & Taylor's Birdcage restaurants.**
Design: Raymond Loewy/William Snaith Incorporated; *Illustrator*: José M. Reinares Méndez

These are contemporary renderings of typical Communist-era architecture constructed in Poland. Hard stone surfaces are indicated by making them reflective. Every wall is rendered to carefully indicate the textural quality of the material. Pawel Hardej, then an architecture student in Warsaw, now lives and works in the United States.

FIGURE 6.27 Lobby and entrance hall, the Palace of Culture and Science, Warsaw, Poland, 1955.

Illustrator: Pawel Hardej; *Media*: Mixed

FIGURE 6.28 Lobby and entrance hall, the Palace of Culture and Science, Warsaw, Poland, 1955.

Illustrator: Pawel Hardej; *Media*: Mixed

CHAPTER SEVEN

1960 to 1969

The first half of the 1960s was a time of optimism and consumerism. The American economy was healthy and expanding. Construction of apartment houses and garden apartment developments was booming. Suburban tract houses were filled with baby boomers growing up. People had more discretionary income than ever before. Especially in America, this was being spent on such items as cars, second homes, boats, and travel.

During the Kennedy years, the restoration of several famous White House rooms brought many thousands of visitors to 1600 Pennsylvania Avenue for public tours. They listened to explanations of the provenance of exquisitely crafted pieces of furniture made before the founding of our republic in Newport, Philadelphia, New York, and Baltimore. Jacqueline Kennedy was actively involved with restoring the grandeur of the White House (Fig. 7.1) and worked closely with such designers as Sister Parish, who was responsible for refurbishing the yellow and white drawing room.

Mrs. Kennedy also organized a committee to renovate Blair House, the nation's official guest house in Washington. Private subscriptions paid for the renovation and refurbishing which was carried out by professional designers. McMillen Inc., New York, handled the redecorating of six rooms, including the Lincoln Room, the Blair-Lee double drawing room, and the King's Bedroom.

Interest in fine and applied art was developed at many levels, from abstract expressionist canvases to supergraphics, from prints to posters, from sculptural coffeemakers to ultrasleek place settings. Designer products began to figure strongly in the marketing of contemporary products: Alexander Girard table settings, the Georg Jensen line of products for the home and entertaining, and Marimekko decorative and apparel fabrics all carried a new cachet.

Inventive antiquing proved that professionals starting out on their own could mix and match and not break any design rules. Knockdown furniture could be assembled with screwdrivers and other basic tools. Architect

Benjamin Thompson founded the first Design Research store in a landmark glass building of his design near Harvard Square in Cambridge, Massachusetts. It soon became a mecca for the cognoscenti to purchase contemporary domestic and imported furnishings with confidence that they were investing in good design.

The teenager evolved into a viable economic purchasing category. London's Carnaby Street became a style icon, identifying with everything "pop"—pop music, pop art, pop design. The latter embodied fun, bright, affordable, and readily available products. Reproductions of prints and posters by popular artists such as Roy Lichenstein, Andy Warhol, and Jasper Johns appeared in reception areas, hospital corridors, and dormitory rooms.

New plastics, such as polypropylene, foam rubber, and stretch jersey upholstery fabrics, were translated into furniture and furnishings. Clear plastic seating and tables, chairs of injection-molded polypropylene, foam-rubber blocks carved into abstract forms and covered with brightly colored fabric, and shiny vinyl or metallic wallcoverings gained wide acceptance with both single young professionals (empty nesters) and growing families with preschoolers and teenagers.

Design journals and design journalism flourished. *American Home*, *House Beautiful*, and *House & Garden* were the largest circulation shelter magazines and powerful arbiters of taste; they spearheaded manufacturer and retailer tie-ins to promote products and design talent. More artistic photographic interpreters of interiors, and technical advancements in color photographic film printing made the glossy pages of the shelter monthlies more accurate and appealing.

House and garden tours—from renovated brownstones in Brooklyn Heights to rose gardens in Winnetka—began to appear with regularity on weekend calendars in newspapers across the country. Often sponsored by nonprofit or other public-service groups, the tours help to raise money for worthy causes. At the same time, they gave tour-goers a chance to see pages from the shelter magazines come alive and provided a valuable three-dimensional frame of reference for judging high-quality interior design.

Those who favored more traditional interiors had a broad range of interpreters to select from. Top U.S. furniture manufacturers like Henredon, Baker, and Tomlinson marketed collections that brought reproductions such as those inspired by the Williamsburg restoration. Pieces from French, English, Federal, and Early American model rooms displayed in museums were within the reach of American consumers. Baker's French Country and English Country collections were meticulously researched and presented in full-room settings.

Interior architecture gained a strong foothold as a blending of the organization of interior spaces for commercial use, the appropriate mechanical and electronic systems, and the interior furnishings needed to support an efficient work force.

Interiors began to reflect an image—private, corporate, or institutional environments were the new genre of serious interiors planned and conceived by trained professionals who worked from programs that were developed with the client to provide the designers with data on the tasks to be carried out in the space. Furnishings and equipment were specified to make the work spaces functional and efficient.

Ellen Lehman McCluskey's interior design firm produced beautifully composed public spaces for restaurants, lobbies, and boardrooms. Firms such as Tom Lee, Dorothy Draper, David Hicks, and Raymond Loewy/William Snaith were leaders in the design of hotels, public spaces, and restaurants. In-house design departments were established by large corporations to introduce quality control and monitor the corporate design standards in branch offices and other support and manufacturing facilities around the United States and overseas.

Retail store planning and design became a subspecialty, combining the philosophies of merchandising, traffic-generating exteriors, and product-enhancing interiors. Chain and multiple stores required designs that could be repeated for speed and cost savings, and modified as appropriate for regional and community variations.

Lighting design became an independent design specialty. Once carried out primarily by electrical engineers who provided the power and illumination that met safety and technical criteria, lighting designers also introduced aesthetics, psychology, and special effects. Fixtures for residential and commercial use became more sophisticated and integrated into the overall interior plan.

For the professional designer, *Interiors*, *Interior Design*, and *Contract* (now *Contract Design*) provided design ideas from top practitioners, product knowledge, and technical advisories. Award programs sponsored by professional organizations such as the American Institute of Architects (AIA), the American Society of Interior Designers (ASID), the design journals, and product producers continue to focus attention on high-quality design and innovative designers.

The second half of the decade was more sober by contrast. The impact of the Kennedy and King assassinations and the escalating war in Vietnam was felt in the United States and overseas. Hippies and flower children became an antimaterialistic counterculture. Adaptations of the casual lifestyle appeared as piles of pillows or cushions on the floor instead of chairs; beds were covered in natural fiber throws.

Expo '67 in Montreal attracted pavilions from countries worldwide. The U.S. pavilion was housed in a geodesic dome, an innovation of the inventor/designer R. Buckminster Fuller.

Holiday cards decorated with a drawing of a beautiful White House room have been repeated several times since first sent by President and Mrs. Kennedy in 1962. The drama of the Red Room is accented with slanted brush strokes applied with several crisp values of black-and-white paint. The needlepoint carpet is loosely rendered. (*Courtesy of Historic Hudson Valley, Tarrytown, New York.*)

With our appreciation and best wishes for a happy Christmas
1962

FIGURE 7.1   Holiday card, 1962, commissioned by President John F. Kennedy and First Lady Jacqueline Kennedy, showing the Red Room of the White House. This limited edition card was sent to the White House staff and the Kennedy's personal list.
Illustrator: Ed Lehman; *Medium*: Gouache

Elizabeth Hoopes is rightly acknowledged as one of America's most talented room portraitists. Her trained artist's eye and sensitive ability to skillfully capture the composition of a room elevate her work to a special niche in the art of room illustration.

Ms. Hoopes expertly utilizes clear, clean washes to present a variety of materials—zebra-patterned rugs, sheer curtains, oriental carpets, needlepoint pillows, furry afghan throws, shiny damask upholstery fabric, an impressionist painting, and a red lacquer console. Use of textures make them seem real. Color and light infuse her paintings.

FIGURE 7.2 **Portrait of a living room, 1961.**
Design: McMillen Inc.; *Illustrator*: Elizabeth Hoopes;
Medium: Watercolor

FIGURE 7.3 **Portrait of a living room, 1961.**
Design: McMillen Inc.; *Illustrator*: Elizabeth Hoopes;
Medium: Watercolor

Elizabeth Hoopes plays strong darks against the bright white of the paper itself to create form and contrast.

FIGURE 7.4   **Living room.**
Design: McMillen Inc.; *Illustrator*: Elizabeth Hoopes; *Medium*: Watercolor

FIGURE 7.5   **Study, 1961.**
Design: McMillen Inc.; *Illustrator*: Elizabeth Hoopes; *Medium*: Watercolor

Two very different expressions of interior design styles are here interpreted by Nadim Racy. The formal living room scheme, unified by the gray and off-white tones of walls, fabrics, and rug, is crisply and lightly rendered. The sheen of the polished parquet flooring is seen as a border. Walls and window coverings are pale and act as background foil for the room's furnishings.

Mr. Racy's drawing for this predominantly ochre and white foyer on the left was completed after he had joined the influential New York City design firm headed by Ellen McCluskey, whose practice included residences and commercial projects. His treatment of the mixed patterns on the walls and the area rug glows with sunlight from the window on the right. In the foreground, a flowering plant in its wicker basket adds a joyful, springtime note to this elegant entry.

FIGURE 7.6   Entrance foyer for a New York City apartment, c. late 1960s.
Design: Ellen McCluskey Associates; *Illustrator*: Nadim Racy; *Medium*: Gouache

FIGURE 7.7   Model living room, W. & J. Sloane, New York City, c. early 1960s.
Illustrator: Nadim Racy; *Medium*: Gouache

John Braden was appointed a member of the design staff of Baker Furniture Company, Grand Rapids, Michigan, in 1963. Mr. Braden's specialty was eighteenth-century furniture; he had headed his own design studio in New York and was also associated with Lord & Taylor and several New York interiors firms before joining Baker. He interpreted the original pieces of European and British furniture for introduction into Baker's lines of handcrafted reproductions. An accomplished artist, he painted the room settings that he created for the Baker showrooms.

"Mr. Braden's illustrations have a definite European feel. His particular palette and his very unique personal style give these illustrations a special character all their own." (Alex W. Mitchell, director of Creative Services, Baker Furniture.) Figures 7.8 through 7.12 are drawings of showrooms created for Baker Furniture during the 1960s.

Baker Furniture, one of the most admired of American furniture makers, has over the years presented many lines of authentic reproductions from some of the richest historical periods in furniture history, starting with its Old World Collection of 1931. Mr. Braden, who combined a designer's creativity with an artist's drawing skill, illustrated his showrooms for the Baker catalog, employing a charming freehand, loose style using pen-and-ink line and muted colors.

FIGURE 7.8 **Living room, English Country Collection, Baker Furniture Company.**
Design and illustration: John Braden; *Medium:* Watercolor

FIGURE 7.9 **Conversation corner, French Country Collection, Baker Furniture Company.**
Design and illustration: John Braden; *Medium:* Watercolor

FIGURE 7.10　**Living room, French Country Collection, Baker Furniture Company.**
Design and illustration: John Braden; *Medium*: Watercolor

FIGURE 7.11   Dining room, French Country Collection, Baker Furniture Company.
Design and illustration: John Braden; *Medium*: Watercolor

FIGURE 7.12   Bedroom, English Country Collection, Baker Furniture Company.
Design and illustration: John Braden; *Medium*: Watercolor

Figures 7.13 and 7.14 are room paintings, 1961.

The works of artist Elizabeth Hoopes bring the painterly quality of light filling her compositions, seeming to radiate simultaneously from many surfaces. Her painting of the green and white dining room (Fig. 7.13) links the leafiness of the tree outside the window with the wall covering pattern.

The bedroom vignette (Fig. 7.14) captures the softness and textures of the fabrics of the window treatment, the skirted table, and the tufted chairs, with a suggestion of the green, white, and rose patterned area carpet in the foreground.

FIGURE 7.13 **Dining room.**
Design: McMillen Inc.; *Illustrator*: Elizabeth Hoopes; *Medium*: Watercolor

FIGURE 7.14 **Vignette, bed/sitting room.**
Design: McMillen Inc.; *Illustrator*: Elizabeth Hoopes; *Medium*: Watercolor

For this sleek, modern living room, designer Marianne Willisch used a controlled pencil line for textural effect for the wood-framed furniture and built-in benches, carpet, and window coverings. Other contemporary furnishings chosen for the room include chrome and glass tables and wire-base seating. She gave importance to the abstract artworks on the rear wall and the sculptures on the benches. (*Estate of Marianne Willisch, 1984.1258.1. Photo: ©1993, The Art Institute of Chicago.*)

FIGURE 7.15 **Living room of an apartment, c. 1965.**
Design: Marianne Willisch and Sigmund Edestone; *Illustrator*: Marianne Willisch;
Media: Pencil, colored pencil, and collage on white tracing paper

Robert L. Sutton worked in a variety of media—oil, transparent watercolor, acrylic, gouache, marker, and casein—to produce a large body of work originally commissioned by his architectural and industrial clients. Here, he chose a one-point perspective to convey the strong vertical lines of this proposed lobby. Areas of bright primary color against off-white emphasize the modern architectural space. (*The Drawings Collection, College of Architecture, Lawrence Technological University, Southfield, Michigan. Photo:* © *Suzanne E. Nicholson.*)

FIGURE 7.16   **Office building lobby, c. 1960.**
Design: Giffels Associates; *Illustrator:* Robert L. Sutton;
Media: Marker and watercolor wash

Emphasis on the carpet pattern and decorative wall treatments are strong selling points for the designer when presenting renderings of commercial spaces to clients. Chairs and chandeliers are also important elements in the overall presentation of spaces such as this cocktail lounge and dining room. To delineate the many tables and chairs in correct perspective is a challenge to the illustrator, artistically executed in this drawing by Robert Martin.

FIGURE 7.17   **Bar in a country club, c. 1960s.**
Design: McMillen Inc.; *Illustrator:* Robert Martin;
Medium: Tempera

FIGURE 7.18 **Dining room in a country club, c. 1960s.**
Design: McMillen Inc.; *Illustrator*: Robert Martin; *Medium*: Tempera

Repetition of geometric forms, here the circular motif on the chair backs and dividers along the window wall, is an identifying theme of the 1960s. Illustrator Nadim Racy's crisp handling of the white and red seating and table and bar surfaces stand out in relief against the looser technique he used to suggest the exposed ceiling grid, carpet pattern, and the curved window framing.

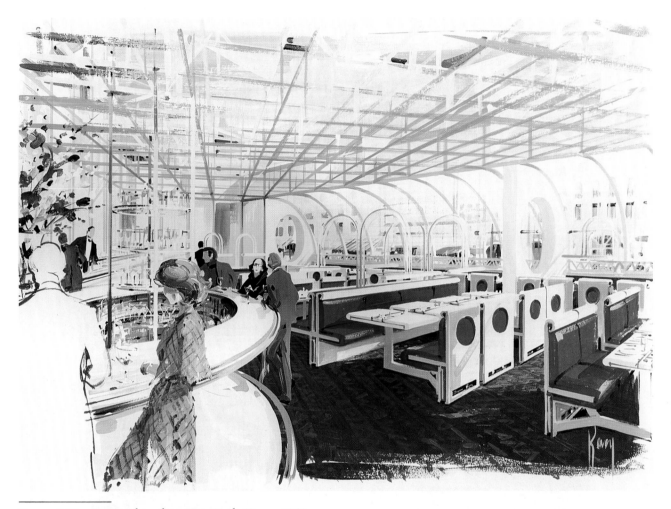

FIGURE 7.19 **Design for a bar, New York City, c. 1960s.**
Design: Ellen McCluskey Associates; *Illustrator*: Nadim Racy; *Medium*: Gouache

Nadim Racy depicted four traders sharing each freestanding white workstation. An electronic quotation board hangs below a mirrored panel that is suspended from the wood-beamed ceiling.

FIGURE 7.20   **Trading room, American Stock Exchange, New York City, 1968.**
Design: Ellen McCluskey Associates; *Illustrator:* Nadim Racy; *Medium:* Acrylic

The artist chose a high, central viewpoint to emphasize the grand expanse of this exposition space. The white tapered mast of the yacht in the foreground carries the eye upward from the floor displays to the dark-toned ceiling. Through the window mullions can be seen the skyline of Chicago and its landmark buildings, giving the drawing a distinguishable sense of place. (*Gift of Helmut Jahn, 1982.1081. Photo: ©1993, The Art Institute of Chicago.*)

FIGURE 7.21   **Interior perspective view of the Exposition Center at McCormick Place, Chicago, Illinois, 1969.**
Design: C. F. Murphy and Associates; *Media*: Ink and watercolor on board

John R. Blackwell has specialized in the rendering of commercial spaces. He is a designer as well as a gifted illustrator, and has a sure grasp of the current trends in commercial interiors. His renderings interweave attention to detail and polished techniques with a thorough understanding of design.

FIGURE 7.22 **Lunch counter.**
Design: Raymond Loewy/William Snaith; *Illustrator*: John R. Blackwell; *Medium*: Pastel

FIGURE 7.23 **Bar lounge, TWA Terminal, John F. Kennedy Airport, New York, 1969.**
Design: Raymond Loewy/William Snaith; *Illustrator*: John R. Blackwell; *Medium*: Pastel

FIGURE 7.24 **Millinery salon, Rich's, Atlanta, Georgia, 1965.**
Design: Raymond Loewy/William Snaith; *Illustrator*: John R. Blackwell; *Medium*: Pastel

FIGURE 7.25 **Department store beauty salon, 1967.**
Design: Raymond Loewy/William Snaith; *Illustrator*: John R. Blackwell; *Medium*: Pastel

Renderers of commercial spaces stress colors in their drawings to help sell the design. Colored surfaces of merchandise can occupy up to 50 percent of the drawing's surface, so its presentation can be critical to the design's acceptance. Here, Buddy Leahy added brightly attired shoppers to accent the fashionable merchandise and environment.

FIGURE 7.26   **Linen and bath department for a department store, 1968.**
Illustrator: Buddy Leahy; *Medium*: Watercolor

Produced for the architectural firm for which he then worked, Robert L. Sutton used a single warm tan color to define the courtroom design, with the wood-paneled walls and bases of the jurors' curved table and other customized furnishings. Figures are silhouetted in the foreground and lightly outlined in the background where the design elements are dominant. (*The Drawings Collection, College of Architecture, Lawrence Technological University, Southfield, Michigan. Photo:* © *Suzanne E. Nicholson.*)

FIGURE 7.27   **Courtroom, c. 1960.**
Design: Giffels Associates;
Illustrator: Robert L. Sutton;
Media: Marker on board

The unfolding drama of this classic film looms in the ombré shadowing of the curving stairway that dominates this view. Visible at the top of the drawing is a chandelier which casts the large ominous shadow behind the woman on the stair landing. (*Margaret Herrick Library, Leo "K" Kuter Collection, Academy Foundation, Beverly Hills, California. Courtesy of Kay E. Kuter.*)

FIGURE 7.28   Center hall of the Flood home, *The Dark at the Top of the Stairs,* Warner Brothers, 1960, starring Robert Preston, Dorothy McGuire, Angela Lansbury, and Eve Arden. (Delbert Mann, director; Leo "K" Kuter, art director.)

Media: Pencil and watercolor on board

By employing a minimal drawing technique, the unmistakable drama of this space is actually heightened. The sound that would be produced by the exposed organ pipes seems to be directed upward through the ceiling opening in this perspective. Light shading at the ceiling and deeper slanted shadows against the front wall highlight architect Weese's design. (*Gift of Harry Weese and Associates, 1982.763. Photo: ©1993, The Art Institute of Chicago. All rights reserved.*)

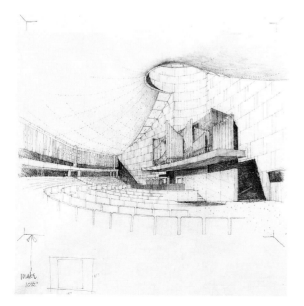

FIGURE 7.29   Interior perspective, Seventeenth Church of Christ, Scientist, Chicago, Illinois, c. 1968.

Design: Harry Weese and Associates;

Media: Graphite and white crayon or oil pastel on tracing paper

CHAPTER EIGHT

1970 *to* 1979

The decade of the 1970s was the start of *big design*, referring not to the scale of the furnishings of interior spaces, but more to the size, influence, and geographical reach of the firms who were taking over commercial and institutional design. Large, multioffice firms such as Skidmore, Owings, & Merrill (SOM) became prolific and inventive designers on a megascale, extending their responsibility for a structure not only to the planning and design but to the interior finishes and furnishings for highrise office buildings, schools, and municipal buildings. Firms such as Gensler specialized in interior architecture, offering space planning and the fitting-out of occupied and support spaces.

Office design was dominated by the systems furnishings approach. Ever since the mid-1960s when Germany's Quickborner Team brought to the United States their then-radical office layout theories that floor-to-ceiling fixed walls were out and movable partitions and workstations were in, office design became the topic of sociological, psychological, production, and ergonomic arguments. Was the "open plan" concept really more beneficial than the traditional perimeter private offices layout, and, if so, for whom? The CFO? The worker? The facility manager? Spatial and auditory privacy, variations in one's workspace, control—or lack of it—over lighting and temperature levels were discussed at length at conferences and in trade journals.

Office furniture manufacturers Herman Miller Company and Steelcase were pioneers in company-sponsored research and development into the ergonomics of office, laboratory, and health care facility furnishings and equipment. Precepts of environmental psychology were analyzed and selected results of tests and evaluations were made part of the lines of these manufacturers. Office furniture retailers, who in the past were primarily distributors of desks, chairs, filing cabinets, and the like, now found themselves in the office design business as well. Trained interiors specialists were hired and design departments were established by office furniture dealers to assist customers with a total furnishings and accessory package, customized to their own and their company's needs.

Programming became established as a new design service to business and institutional clients. This subdiscipline is based on a structured series of questions and answers to determine how users perceive their tasks, the equipment (furnishings and machines) that they use on a daily basis, and the flow of information and communication within their group, department, and company involved in their job. The objective is to resolve the various ingredients of programmed needs into not only a good-looking result, but to make that result workable.

The Institute of Business Designers was formed in the United States to serve the information interchange and networking needs of designers who practiced in the commercial/institutional market exclusively.

In a time of high competition, the physical facility itself is no small part of the marketing message. The success of the image communicated by a store, bank, or dining establishment depends on how well the owners believe that the design helps to draw the public through the door.

Clients tend to feel more comfortable with design consultants who have a track record of success within a certain industry. Specialists in such areas as store design, hotel design, lounge and restaurant design, have a competitive edge over other practitioners who lack the technical expertise in a certain building/interiors type; clients can spend less in educating the designers about the basics of their business, and more on project specifics.

Discotheques gave designers the opportunity to experiment with special effects with colors, lighting, and finishes to create an environment dedicated to entertainment. "It bathes the patrons nightly in an enchanting, throbbing, mind-bending array of light and sound" is how one design magazine described New York City's Studio 54. "The range of possible lighting effects—effects that heighten the sensation of the dancer as performer—seems almost inexhaustible."

The casual acceptance with which consumers accepted the energy needed to illuminate their homes and places of business was jolted with the decade's first oil crisis. Ambient and specialty lighting sources were now scrutinized for both the quantity of energy needed for illumination and the quality of light required for users to perform their activities. (Discotheques such as those previously described were obviously outside the mainstream of lighting uses.)

States such as California and New York passed legislation mandating acceptable ranges of illumination for various interior spaces, typically measured in watts per square foot, connected load. Designers also integrated into their plans such factors as reflective qualities of colors used on walls and floors; techniques to bring daylighting into the core of a large office floor; and economical, high-output lamps such as metal halide and low voltage multireflector (MR).

Healthy design, the movement that made consumers aware of their diet and personal physical fitness, began to hit its stride in the 1970s. Tennis was ranked number one, and tennis clubs occupied new and renovated facilities around the country.

Gyms and athletic clubs, with and without swimming pools, began to appear in urban areas and in suburban office parks as an employee perk. Bright lighting, bright coloring, and precise hard-edge shapes replaced the dimly lit, gray-metal milieus of the zealous weightlifter.

Malls and marketplaces were the dominant building types for merchandising. Many small and midsize cities struggled to keep intact their once-prosperous downtown commercial centers in the face of overwhelming competition from surrounding suburban malls and shopping centers.

After decades of neglect, the vision of developers such as James Rouse revived the urban marketplace. The architectural firm of Benjamin Thompson & Associates used the appeal of an animated gathering place as a primary attraction to draw business for shops and restaurants. For projects including Boston's Faneuil Hall Marketplace and Baltimore's Harborplace, Rouse and Thompson created the urban "festival" marketplace. They brought new life to sturdy old buildings and triggered the revitalization of both cities' waterfronts.

The era of mass merchandising and mass communication encompassed midprice residential furniture. With baby boomers now starting their own homes, either alone or with a mate, a large market opened up for home furnishings retailers. Affordable and functional contemporary furnishings were available from multistore chains such as British-based Conran's. IKEA's warehouse, assemble-it-yourself approach was successfully imported from Europe and extensively promoted in the United States with heavy advertising and big, glossy mail-order catalogs.

An appreciation for fine food and wines, popularized by such gurus of gourmet as Julia Child, Craig Claiborne, and James Beard, made the kitchen and its built-in and portable equipment a status symbol. Merchants capitalized on the trend by staging in-store events featuring table settings by well-known fashion and interior designers. The separate formal dining room, which had gone into hibernation as a dining "L" in the 1950s and 1960s, made a strong comeback.

Rehab, adaptive reuse, and restoration, for both residential and commercial buildings, began to be recognized in the 1970s as a patriotic gesture that also made good economic sense. With permits for new construction becoming harder to obtain—community hearings, lengthy filing procedures, and stringent environmental approvals made developers dread the process—the approvals required to renovate an existing building often took comparatively less time and effort.

Homeowners and professional developers alike became involved in giving new life to older buildings. Their completed projects ranged from fairly accurate restorations to more liberal interpretations. Entire sections of cities were brought back to life during this period. Philadelphia's Society Hill combined renovated eighteenth- and nineteenth-century townhouses with new low- and high-rise construction. Empty lofts in New York's Soho became live-and-work spaces for artists and professionals. Elegant century-old residential buildings in Boston's South End were modernized and upgraded as single family and multiunit dwellings.

Marker on vellum is a technique that the artist can accomplish quickly as an underdrawing for the placement of furniture. A piece of tracing paper is then placed on top, retraced, and color added. In this way, the renderer eliminates transferring the drawing to illustration board and mixing a painting medium.

Joseph Braswell, who has been elected to membership in the *Interior Design Hall of Fame*, has a varied residential and commercial practice. He has also designed the interiors of several airplanes and oceangoing yachts.

FIGURE 8.1   **Living room in an apartment, Philadelphia, Pennsylvania, 1978.**
Design and illustration: Joseph Braswell, ASID; *Medium*: Felt marker on vellum

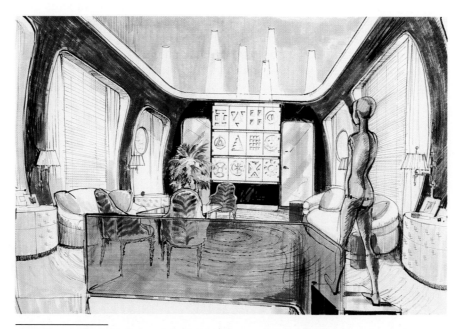

FIGURE 8.2   **Main salon of a yacht, 1972.**
Design and illustration: Joseph Braswell, ASID; *Medium*: Felt marker on vellum

Masterful illustrator Nadim Racy captured the sleek look of the 1970s in these two drawings. For Fig. 8.3, the perspective of the checkerboard-patterned floor directs the viewer's attention to the molded-foam seating, Oriental-style chairs and screen, and clear plastic cube table. In Fig. 8.4, Mr. Racy captured the élan of Ellen McCluskey's own all-white living room accented with red lacquer walls, a 1970s version of British decorator Syrie Maugham's 1929–1930 all-white drawing room for her London home.

FIGURE 8.3 **Living room, New York City, 1972.**
Design: Ellen McCluskey Associates; *Illustrator*: Nadim Racy;
Medium: Watercolor

FIGURE 8.4 **Living room of interior designer Ellen McCluskey's New York City apartment, 1974.**
Design: Ellen McCluskey Associates; *Illustrator*: Nadim Racy; *Medium*: Gouache

Four different progressions of space are depicted in Fig. 8.5—living room, dining room, piano alcove, and the outdoors beyond the sliding glass doors. Crisp, clean grays against the white of the paper make this modern living room sparkle. The details of the telescope, chandelier, and the sculpture add to the setting's artistic balance.

FIGURE 8.5 **Living room, Harbour Front Apartments, Toronto, Canada, 1977.**
Design: Csagoly, Miller Interior Design; *Illustrator*: Michael McCann; *Medium*: Watercolor

To enliven this gray, white, and gold room, slanting rays of sunlight through the casement draperies are reflected on the clear plastic accent pieces and against the wall. The pattern of the wall covering, which is actually an overall design, is partially indicated in this rendering.

FIGURE 8.6 **Model living room in Seven Corners Condominium, Falls Church, Virginia, 1972.**
Design: W. & J. Sloane (Sarah B. Jenkins, ASID); *Illustrator*: Elizabeth McClure Wolfson; *Medium*: Watercolor

The proposed vice-presidential residence in Quarters "A" of the U.S. Naval Observatory in Washington, D.C., had a blue and gold color scheme and classic furniture and accessories. This view calls attention to the semicircular alcove and the patterned carpet in the foreground.

FIGURE 8.7   Living areas and reception hall for former Vice President Gerald Ford and family, vice-presidential residence, Washington, D.C., 1975.

Design: Ken Murray (Department of the Navy, Chesapeake Division); *Illustrator*: Elizabeth McClure Wolfson; *Medium*: Watercolor

Albert Hadley's spare sketch style gives clients insight into the originality of his designs. His quick evocative line drawings have previewed his tasteful interiors for over four decades.

FIGURE 8.8   **Living room, New York City, 1979.**
Design: Parish-Hadley Associates (Albert Hadley);
Illustrator: Albert Hadley, FASID; *Medium*: Felt-tip pen

FIGURE 8.9   **Drawing room, New York City, 1979.**
Design: Parish-Hadley Associates (Albert Hadley);
Illustrator: Albert Hadley, FASID; *Medium*: Felt-tip pen

FIGURE 8.10   **Dining Room, New York City, 1979.**
Design: Parish-Hadley Associates (Albert Hadley);
Illustrator: Albert Hadley, FASID; *Medium*: Felt-tip pen

The night sky, visible through the full-length glass doors and windows, adds richness to the deep tones of the furniture and the window wall of this elegant urban apartment.

FIGURE 8.11   **Night view, living room, 1970s.**
Design: Yale R. Burge, ASID; *Illustrator*: Robert Martin; *Media*: Watercolor and gouache

The late Yale R. Burge achieved success both as an interior designer and as a furniture manufacturer and distributor. His signature style—French and English period reproduction pieces combined with contemporary furnishings and a bold accent color palette—were given lively interpretations by illustrator Robert Martin.

For Fig. 8.12, Mr. Martin employed the technique of a dark nighttime view outside for contrast as in Fig. 8.11, and emphasized the brightly lit white-walled rooms. Figure 8.13 is an opaque painting on blueprint paper. The green secretary is strikingly placed against a dark blue wall, minimally highlighted with a few accents of light tones to create contrast. For the dining room in Fig. 8.14, Mr. Martin created interest in the chairs by assigning them different angles, a renderer's technique applied to situations where elements repeat. Slashes of brush strokes represent light and shadow. Geometric and floral patterns of the brick wall, wallpaper, and carpet are interplayed for textural interest.

FIGURE 8.12   **Living room in an urban high-rise, c. 1970s.**
Design: Yale R. Burge Reproductions; *Illustrator*: Robert Martin; *Media*: Watercolor and gouache

FIGURE 8.13 **Setting with chair and secretary for American Society of Interior Designers show, Atlanta, Georgia, 1976.**
Design: Yale R. Burge Reproductions; *Illustrator*: Robert Martin; *Media*: Watercolor and gouache

FIGURE 8.14 **Dining room, c. 1970s.**
Design: Yale R. Burge Reproductions; *Illustrator*: Robert Martin; *Media*: Watercolor and gouache

The expansion and renovation programs of the 1970s undertaken by major hotel/motel chains were aimed at attracting business travelers and tourists alike. Elizabeth McClure Wolfson's presentation gave this typical guest room a visual personality by vignetting the foreground and adding broad highlights for the ceiling and walls.

FIGURE 8.15 **Typical guest room, Old Town Holiday Inn, Alexandria, Virginia, 1975.**
Design: Design IV (Susan Fraley); *Illustrator*: Elizabeth McClure Wolfson; *Medium*: Watercolor

Geometric supergraphics, dark walls and carpet, and fitted bedding were typical style features of 1970s bedroom interiors.

FIGURE 8.16   Model bedroom in Seven Corners Condominium, Falls Church, Virginia, 1972.

Design: W. & J. Sloane (Sarah B. Jenkins, ASID); *Illustrator*: Elizabeth McClure Wolfson; *Medium*: Watercolor

Designers—consciously and subconsciously—draw their inspiration from many sources. For this child's bedroom, the designer may have been influenced by fabric patterns and built-in seating and daybeds originating in the century's early decades.

FIGURE 8.17   Children's bedroom, Washington, D.C.–area residence, 1972.

Design: W. & J. Sloane (Victor Shargai, ASID); *Illustrator*: Elizabeth McClure Wolfson; *Medium*: Watercolor

The late Buddy Leahy's illustrations, like the artist himself, were characterized by an overall sparkle, a positive attitude, and a patrician sense of style.
Figures 8.18 through 8.22 are renderings by Buddy Leahy, c. 1978–1979.

FIGURE 8.18   Buddy added width to this narrow kitchen by integrating the white paper surface as a background into the composition to indicate sunlight falling onto surfaces.
Media: Watercolor and gouache

FIGURE 8.19   Strategically placed areas of gold tones communicate a festive, gala feel to this cocktail lounge. The ceiling softly reflects the room's design elements.
Media: Watercolor and gouache

FIGURE 8.20   A floor of highly polished white marble provides a dramatic surface for a lobby rendered in soft hues.

Illustrator: Buddy Leahy; *Media*: Watercolor and gouache

FIGURE 8.21   Buddy Leahy could vary his style to best impart the personality of the space he was presenting. Here, he utilized a loose, broad brush technique for this large lobby with multiple seating areas, triple windows, two chandeliers, and patterned walls and furniture coverings.

Illustrator: Buddy Leahy; *Media*: Watercolor and gouache

FIGURE 8.22   For the strong architectural impression of this multilevel lobby, Buddy's style tightened, and the carefully detailed geometry was the dominant theme. The streams of cascading water are beautifully rendered, adding to the strong verticality of the space.

Illustrator: Buddy Leahy; *Media*: Watercolor and gouache

A superb control of pencil tone and texture and dramatic use of shadows to delineate architectural form are Paul Stevenson Oles' graphic signature. He has translated many of architect I. M. Pei's ideas into renderings, choosing perspectives that convey the dimensional power and the intellectual concepts behind the designs.

The atrium lobby rendering of the proposed Asia House captured the sweep of the curved forms in the foreground and on the left, and the rhythm of the rectangular openings of right-hand balconies, and the glass panels of the facade facing existing surrounding structures.

FIGURE 8.23 **Asia House, New York City (not constructed), 1975.**
Design: I. M. Pei & Partners; *Illustrator*: Paul Stevenson Oles, FAIA; *Medium*: Black Prismacolor on vellum (with underlay)

This Escher-like drawing is a visual tour de force of 1970s earthtones and geo-metric patterns. Atop an upholstered banquette in the foreground is a trans-parent plastic header, suggesting a surface for patrons to place their drinks. The designers placed mirrored vertical partitions between built-in seating areas.

FIGURE 8.24 Cocktail lounge, Royal Bank Plaza, Toronto, Canada, 1974.
Design: Louis Kareny Interiors; *Illustrator*: Michael McCann; *Medium*: Watercolor

The sheen and glisten of the metal chandeliers above this boardroom confer-
ence table is an example of employing visual license to vary the rendering of a
long wood surface. Broad shadowing lends texture to the fabric-covered surfaces of the board members' chairs.

FIGURE 8.25   Corporate boardroom, Englewood,
New Jersey, c. 1978.
Design: Thomas V. Di Carlo/Shepard Martin
Associates; *Illustrator*: Caroline Halliday;
Media: Mixed

The distinctive, sophisticated ambience of the Palm Court is unmistakable in
this Nadim Racy rendering.

FIGURE 8.26   Palm Court, Plaza Hotel,
New York City, 1976.
Design: Ellen McCluskey Associates;
Illustrator: Nadim Racy; *Medium*: Acrylic

Dancers and diners are reflected in both the mirrored dance floor and the dropped illuminated mirrored ceiling. Nadim Racy captured the dynamics of the setting for this swank disco nightclub. Compare this interpretation with Joseph Urban's drawing of The Roof Garden of the Hotel Gibson in Cincinnati (Fig. 3.38).

FIGURE 8.27   Discotheque, New York City, c. 1970s.

Design: Ellen McCluskey Associates; *Illustrator:* Nadim Racy; *Medium:* Acrylic

One of the era's premier fashion illustrators combined sleek merchandise presentation with architectural backdrops.

FIGURE 8.28   Drawing for Bonwit Teller's newspaper advertising and brochures, c. 1970s.
Illustrator: J. Hyde Crawford;
Medium: Charcoal on paper

FIGURE 8.29   Drawing for Bonwit Teller's newspaper advertising and brochures, c. 1970s.
Illustrator: J. Hyde Crawford;
Medium: Charcoal on paper

Paul Stevenson Oles' distinctive renditions capture the bold curves and sweeping planes within this atrium lobby that features a space frame roof and facade. His human figures, positioned throughout the multilevel space, are shown in less detail than the architecture, a subtle visual technique that keeps the viewer's interest on the structure's design objectives.

FIGURE 8.30   Wilson Commons, University of Rochester, Rochester, New York, 1972.
Design: I. M. Pei & Partners;
Illustrator: Paul Stevenson Oles, FAIA;
Medium: Black Prismacolor on vellum

FIGURE 8.31   Oakland University Library, Oakland, California, 1972.

Design: BEI; *Illustrator*: Robert L. Sutton; *Medium*: Felt marker on illustration board

(*The Drawings Collection, College of Architecture, Lawrence Technological University.*)

FIGURE 8.32   General Motors test laboratory, 1970.

Design: BEI; *Illustrator*: Robert L. Sutton; *Medium*: Gouache

(*The Drawings Collection, College of Architecture, Lawrence Technological University.*)

CHAPTER NINE

Dubbed by media pundits as the "Go-Go 80s," the decade peaked on lavishness, liberal spending, and high-visibility luxuries. The fine art market went out of sight. The upward curve of the residential real estate market showed no obvious signs of flattening. Office buildings were comfortably rented-up in major metropolitan areas and in suburban office parks. Designers were called on to create distinctive interiors for yachts and private jets.

1980 to 1989

Facilities that serve the travel and entertainment industries were busy with new construction or expansion programs. These included casinos, dining establishments, theaters and multimedia centers, and hotels.

The wealthy rulers of Mideast oil countries engaged the services of top designers from around the world to provide family living environments within their palaces. Communism was giving way to capitalism in the Soviet Union and the Eastern Block. Designs coming off the drawing board (manual or electronic) ranged from television centers to hotels.

When the stock market went into its deep nosedive in October 1987, it triggered a worldwide recession. Its effects were felt in many areas of the design world.

"Vienna 1900: Art, Architecture & Design" was organized in 1986 by the Museum of Modern Art in New York. This dazzling presentation covered approximately the period before and after the turn of the century when Vienna was driven by the creative energies of its writers, artists, architects, designers, and craftspeople.

"The Machine Age in America: 1918–1941" captured the mood and energy of an age in transition, the years between the two world wars when the machine was the principle motivating force, heralding a whole new way of life. It featured examples of the work of many of the artists and designers shown in this book, including Hugh Ferriss, Henry Dreyfuss, Raymond Loewy, Le Corbusier, Holabird and Root. Sketches by Frank Lloyd Wright and scenes from a Busby Berkeley film were among the hundreds of items displayed.

"The Treasure Houses of Britain" exhibition drew throngs to the National Gallery of Art in Washington, D.C., in 1986. Choice examples of chinoiserie, porcelain, chairs, cabinets, silver, and paintings and sculpture were on view. Today, more than 850 grand British manor houses and country estates are now entirely or partially opened to the public for tours; some estates and portions of others have been made into hotels, receiving guests in the summer months or year-round.

Computer art became a whole new genre of artistic expression. A by-product of the proliferating visualization techniques, computer art became the first new medium since the invention of the camera in 1839. Computer art shows became accepted in and sponsored by galleries and museums. The exhibition, "Computers and Vision," organized by the Everson Museum of Art, Syracuse University, was on view in late 1987 and 1988 with examples of work by fine artists who were using new computer hardware and software capabilities to create new artistic images. Included in the show were works by the architectural firm of Skidmore, Owings & Merrill. According to the catalog description, "SOM's computer research has recently developed to such an extent that the architectural models are now cut out by a computer driven laser cutter following instructions input from the SOM CAD system. In this way very elaborate models can be constructed with much more accuracy and detail than when they are cut by hand."

Figure 9.41, "Interior View of Addition to the Louvre (from the Pyramid Looking into the Court Napoleon)," produced in 1986, was also in this exhibition. Created by a plotter drawing and felt-tip pen on paper with pencil, its original size was 18 × 22 inches, and was produced by using a Digital Equipment Corporation MicroVAX computer, Tektronix display, with software from McDonnell Douglas GDS edition 4.6. "By combining the computer-generated drawing with a traditional rendering of the site, both the architect and client are given a very exact idea of what the finished building will look like," the catalog noted.

In communities of all sizes, attending art shows and gallery openings carries both a social and aesthetic appeal. Art fairs and art exhibits, held out-of-doors, in townhouses, or in renovated brick-walled streetfront spaces, offer art of all vintages and prices for collectors.

Decorator showhouses are sponsored by charities or institutions and run for a week or more. Typically, an entire empty residence is used, and leading decorators and design firms are invited to create design rooms, usually stunning in their theme and execution. House and garden tours, often run by not-for-profit or charity groups, allow the public to see tasteful and handsome private homes, terraces, and gardens. They offer a three-dimensional version of the popular shelter magazines that target every aspect of lifestyle from *Country Living* to *Metropolitan Home*.

Antique shows, country fairs, flea markets, auctions, weekend outdoor gatherings of dealers in collectibles are great for browsing, comparing, trading, or buying. Catalogs published by the major auction houses for significant sales are excellent visual documentations of private collections or historical periods.

The personal computer, which started the decade as a number-crunching and data-digesting appendage for the techy crowd, dropped dramatically in size and price. As the final decade of the century approached, computers appeared in places of business, in residences from the home office to kids' bedrooms, and in briefcases. The furnishings market responded with an array of electronic-compatible accessories and furniture: chairs, tables, and special space-saving furniture to stack printer, keyboard, and screen units.

Space planning moved from the drawing board to the computer screen. System furniture and the open office concept remained the floor plan of choice for firms of all sizes. Flexibility in arrangement and cost-effective use of space were pointed out as the leading benefits to corporate and institutional users.

Open plan systems with built-in wire management features and ergonomic influences gave the office worker and the knowledge worker work stations to perform their duties within demountable partitions. The biggest drawback? Lack of privacy. Even with high-tech sound-absorbing materials, open plan office occupants often feel that any voice interchange above whisper-level is like sending their conversation out over the wire services.

Merchants and developers were making sure that the customer was entertained during their shopping outings. The 5.2-million-square-foot West Edmonton Mall, Edmonton, Alberta, Canada, is the equivalent of 115 football fields. To go along with its 800 shops and services, there is a professional-size skating rink, a 560,000-square-foot Fantasyland, a Fantasyland Hotel, and several submarines which cruise the 400-foot-long Lake of the Deep.

In Bloomington, Minnesota, construction began on a second North American megamall, the Mall of America. It offers 400 retail stores, 18 theaters, restaurants, nightclubs, a walk-through aquarium, and a 300,000-square-foot Knott's Camp Snoopy.

A $100 million renovation of Marshall Field's venerable State Street store in Chicago introduced new building systems and merchandising concepts to the landmark 1892 building, designed by D. H. Burnham and Company. Across the street, Carson Pirie Scott & Company restored the exterior iron grillwork designed in 1903 by Louis Sullivan, with its double bands of coiling thickets of iron ribbons that extend along State and Madison Streets, massed to form the monumental curved front entrance.

By the 1980s, the majority of American art colleges offered degrees in interior design. In the United States, interior design training had first been offered in 1896 by the New York School of Fine and Applied Art, now known as the Parsons School of Design. In Britain, the profession of interior design became formalized in the late 1960s with the inauguration of tertiary level courses.

In 1986, the American Society of Architectural Perspectivists (ASAP) mounted an annual exhibition, "Architecture in Perspective." The organization broadened its international membership, and the yearly show of top works reflected the work of accomplished practitioners of interior and exterior renderings. According to Thomas Wells Schaller, AIA, an ASAP past president, "Drawing consistently endures as the fundamental way in which to communicate the essence of architecture yet to be built, despite countless changes in technology and the vagaries of economics and the marketplace."

Jeremiah Goodman, a modern master of interior rendering, is one of the most admired practitioners of this art form. Mr. Goodman has set a standard of excellence for nearly four decades that occupies its own stylistic classification. The exuberance of Jeremiah's broad brush strokes and his suggestions of pattern and detail create renderings that are alive with his consistently fresh viewpoint and convey a feeling of expansiveness. Note his wonderful attention to the modern art collection on the wall in this room painting.

FIGURE 9.1 **Living room, Mr. and Mrs. Richard Rodgers, New York City, 1985.**
Design: Dorothy Rodgers; *Illustrator*: Jeremiah Goodman; *Medium*: Gouache

FIGURE 9.2　Library, Mr. and Mrs. Richard Rodgers, New York City, 1984.
Design: Dorothy Rodgers; *Illustrator*: Jeremiah Goodman; *Medium*: Gouache

Caroline Halliday here depicts a warm and welcoming scene, imparted by over-stuffed upholstered pieces and softly rendered chintz and other fabrics. The feeling of diffused shimmering light is created by subtle shading.

FIGURE 9.3 **Living room, prototype for presentation, 1989.**
Illustrator: Caroline Halliday; *Medium*: Watercolor

The use of pen-and-ink, a very precise drawing medium, is used here to indicate the sleekness of a private jet. This view is rendered in one-point perspective, appropriate for showing a long narrow space.

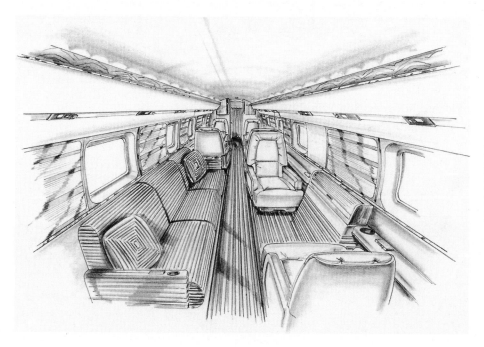

FIGURE 9.4 **Interior for a private jet, 1984.**
Design and illustration: Geoffrey N. Bradfield, Jay Spectre; *Medium*: Pen-and-ink

This painting is held together by the use of soft watercolor washes. The elaborate details of architectural features such as cornices, moldings and the central ceiling medallion are classical reference points. From the dimensional carvings of the decorative console, fireplace, and mantlepiece mirror, to the patterns of the fabrics and carpet, David B. Redmond portrayed a room that respects refined taste. His highly illustrative style includes details down to the brass tacks on the back of the chair on the right.

FIGURE 9.5 **Living room, New York City, 1991.**
Design: Buttrick White & Burtis, Architects; Anthony Hall, interior designer; *Illustrator*: David B. Redmond; *Medium*: Watercolor on board

A fashion illustrator and fabric designer, J. Hyde Crawford's flowing, loose line and bold use of color draw the viewer's eye in and around this composition. The use of white space, often employed in his apparel sketches, is one of this designer's signature stylistic techniques.

FIGURE 9.6 **Living room in a town house, New York City, 1980.**
Design and illustration: J. Hyde Crawford; *Media*: Marker and gouache

Nadim Racy's personal verve and gift of visual communication make him one of the century's most prolific and trendsetting illustrators. His controlled watercolor washes and beautiful use of transparent brush strokes indicate texture and pattern. The delicate treatment of the entourage—plants, paintings, and accessories—balance the larger elements of the setting.

FIGURE 9.7 **Living room, Easthampton, Long Island, New York, 1988.**
Design: Ellen McCluskey Associates; *Illustrator*: Nadim Racy; *Medium*: Acrylic

Light and airy fabrics, accurately rendered, give life to this sun-swept Long Island living room.

FIGURE 9.8 **Living room, Southampton, New York, 1988.**
Design: Michael J. Rosenberg, Incorporated; *Illustrator*: Dani Antman; *Media*: Gouache

Laura Shechter, a contemporary exhibiting painter, takes rendering to a realistic level. Her use of flat color and painterly attention to form and composition express her personal artistic style for this genre.

FIGURE 9.9 **Living room, 1986.**
Artist: Laura Shechter;
Medium: Oil on masonite

This evocative composition plays crisp shades of greens against white and pale neutral tones for a breeze-cooled tropical bayside residence. Buddy Leahy has extended the perspective outside to the balcony and waterway beyond.

FIGURE 9.10 **Master bedroom suite.**
Illustrator: Buddy Leahy; *Media*: Watercolor and gouache

There is no other renderer practicing today who is more adept at the depiction of space-age high-tech forms than Syd Mead. Here, his palette is subdued, against which the reflective surfaces are a stunning contrast.

FIGURE 9.11   **Proposal for the main lounge of a private yacht.**
Design and illustration: Syd Mead, Incorporated; *Medium*: Gouache

Renderings of kitchens can vary from illustrative to painterly. Compare Buddy Leahy's perspective of a kitchen showroom based on white and natural materials with the design style of the 1950s that focused on hard surfaces and bright color laminates.

FIGURE 9.12   **Residential kitchen, 1980s.**
Illustrator: Buddy Leahy; *Media*: Watercolor and gouache

The almost photorealistic attention to detail makes this small bathroom, possibly part of a remodeling of an older home, very lively and imaginative. The tightly framed composition is softened by the sensuous folds of fabric at the ceiling, above the footed tub, and by the pair of peg-hung towels.

This painterly expression of a small apartment kitchen is a study in smoothly integrating a range of materials into a single composition, from the stemware in the cabinets, to the copper teapot on the white enamel stove, to the masonry facade and white metal fire escapes of the buildings seen through the window.

FIGURE 9.14 **"Kitchen on Fillmore I,"** 1985.
Artist: Elizabeth Eve; *Medium*: Oil on canvas

FIGURE 9.13 **Prototype bathroom design,** 1985.
Design: Sunworthy Wallcovering; *Illustrator*: Barbara Morello; *Medium*: Gouache

Michael McCann's overall detailing of this atrium lobby gives viewers a realistic preview of the finished space. Slashing rays of light coming through the clear dome create overhead drama; patterns and light guide the eye through and around the core of this proposed headquarters structure. Colors, by contrast, are soft. The composition is unified by two complementary colors: soft purple-blue and warm yellow-orange.

FIGURE 9.15   **Central atrium, competition for the headquarters of the Canadian Broadcasting Corporation, Toronto, Canada, 1986.**
Design: Zeidler Roberts Partnership; *Illustrator*: Michael McCann; *Medium*: Watercolor

The important image-setting aspect of a speculative office building is often determined by the lobby. Attention here is drawn to the distinctive quality of the architecture, apparent in the materials for the walls, floor, and ceiling. Broad slashes of light coming from windows on the left connect the space with the unseen street.

FIGURE 9.16   Lobby, office building/trading exchange, Bishopsgate, London, England, 1987. *Design*: Skidmore, Owings & Merrill, Chicago, Illinois; *Illustrator*: Rael D. Slutsky & Associates; *Media*: Technical pen and felt-tip pen on vellum with color pencil

Monumental proportions of this landmark space are rendered with consummate skill by Jeremiah Goodman, one of the most admired illustrators of the twentieth century. Using his powers of visual suggestion, he creates a vast interior with light and shadow. Conciseness of detail against unrendered space is expertly balanced, drawing the viewer into the composition with its soaring, complex ceiling.

FIGURE 9.17 **Entry, Stock Exchange Building, Melbourne, Australia, 1986.**
Design: Kalef Alaton; *Illustrator*: Jeremiah Goodman; *Medium*: Gouache

Pier Four, part of Boston's ongoing waterfront revitalization program, is shown here with a transparent roof and entry. Mr. Costantino employs an L-shaped foreground shadow to balance the intricate patterns of the structure flanking the pedestrian walkway and to draw the eye to the atrium's horizontal and vertical elements.

FIGURE 9.18   **Pier Four, Boston, Massachusetts, 1986.**
Design: Kallman, McKinnell & Wood; *Illustrator*: Frank M. Costantino;
Medium: Pencil on illustration paper

Elaborately rendered marble on the floors and the walls characterizes this classically proportioned space.

FIGURE 9.19   **Entry hall for a television center, St. Petersburg, Russia, 1989.**
Design: S. Shmakow, Architect; *Illustrator*: Sergei E. Tchoban; *Medium*: Watercolor

Ernest Fox's lively, loose style establishes a bright, comfortable atmosphere for this executive office.

FIGURE 9.20   Executive office, St. Regis Paper Company, New York City, 1980.
Design: McMillen Inc.; *Illustrator*: Ernest Fox; *Medium*: Tempera

FIGURE 9.21   Executive office, St. Regis Paper Company, New York City, 1980.
Design: McMillen Inc.; *Illustrator*: Ernest Fox; *Medium*: Tempera

FIGURE 9.22   Photo of the final installation of the office shown in Fig. 9.20.
(*Photo: William P. Steele*)

Architect Ricardo Bofill animates this formal architectural drawing by introducing the human form, interpreting the figures as artist's models. (*Collection of the Cooper-Hewitt Museum, New York City, used with permission.*)

FIGURE 9.23   **Mason's Temple.**
Design and illustration: Ricardo Bofill

The multitalented interior designer Angelo Donghia founded a firm to manufacture and distribute fabrics and furniture of his own design and those of other designers.

FIGURE 9.24   **Design for a hotel lobby, 1982.**
Design: Angelo Donghia;
(Illustrator unknown);
Medium: Watercolor

The ambience of these elegant lobbies is interpreted here by two leading illustrators. Both concentrate on delineating the patterns for the floor, ceiling, and furniture with loose applications of color. For the Mayfair Regent lobby, the sparkle of the chandeliers and softness of the ceiling is offset by the broad sweep of arches leading to the seating area beyond. The elaborate luxurious design sparkles because of lively strokes of gouache.

FIGURE 9.25 Main lobby, Waldorf-Astoria Hotel, New York City, 1988.
Design: Kenneth E. Hurd & Associates; *Illustrator*: James Hewson; *Medium*: Gouache

FIGURE 9.26 Mayfair Regent lobby, New York City, 1982.
Design: Ellen McCluskey Associates; *Illustrator*: Nadim Racy; *Medium*: Gouache

Light streaming into this paneled lounge and card room creates a warm and inviting space. The vignetting in the foreground draws the viewer's eye into the room.

FIGURE 9.27　Card room, Mutton-town (New York) Country Club, 1985.
Design: Kiser Gution Quintal; *Illustrator*: Dani Antman; *Medium*: Gouache

This dramatic monotone composition has strong white highlights indicating night lighting in a cocktail lounge setting. Brown tones are skillfully integrated throughout the composition by areas of light and reflections.

FIGURE 9.28　Bar and lounge, New York City, 1988.
Design: Ellen McCluskey Associates; *Illustrator*: Nadim Racy; *Media*: Watercolor and gouache

The late Buddy Leahy's flair and style were well-suited to depicting rooms for dining and entertainment. In these two drawings, he utilizes sheen and reflections to add to the gala mood. He enlivens the supper club in Fig. 9.29 with coffered ceiling details, columns, wall panels, and the textures of the carpeting and dance floor. In Fig. 9.30, mirrors and glass add sparkle to an otherwise muted color palette.

FIGURE 9.29 **Supper club.**
Media: Watercolor and gouache

FIGURE 9.30 **Restaurant interior.**
Design: Jutras & Noboli Associates;
Media: Watercolor and gouache

Figures 9.31 and 9.32 are renderings of a hotel, North Caucasus, Russia, 1989.
The contemporary interpretation of Tudor-period country architecture is the major design element of these rooms and is rendered by Sergei E. Tchoban with stylish effect.

FIGURE 9.31   **Library.**
Design: W. Fabritzkij and Sergei E. Tchoban; *Illustrator*: Sergei E. Tchoban;
Medium: Watercolor

FIGURE 9.32   **Billiards Room.**
Design: W. Fabritzkij and Sergei E. Tchoban; *Illustrator*: Sergei E. Tchoban;
Medium: Watercolor

Mr. Tchoban demonstrates another facet of his technique with this fanciful interpretation of a showcase for apparel designs. Hard surfaces such as marble and brass are tightly rendered, employing various degrees of shading to express surface texture.

FIGURE 9.33   Shop interior, proposed Theatre of Fashion, Moscow, 1989.

Design: A. Shmonkin, S. Zizin, Sergei E. Tchoban; *Illustrator*: Sergei E. Tchoban; *Medium*: Watercolor

The four illustrations on these two pages, Figs. 9.34 through 9.37, are examples of complex renderings and space-age drawings.

FIGURE 9.34   **Proposal for El San Juan Casino, Condado Plaza Hotel, San Juan, Puerto Rico, 1986.**
Illustrator: Prelim (Robert W. Cook); *Medium*: Gouache

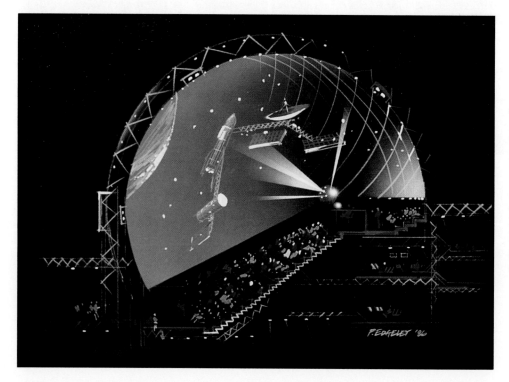

FIGURE 9.35   **Proposed Omni-Max Theatre, Melbourne Central Project, Australia, 1986.**
Design: Kurokawa Architects;
Illustrator: Peter Edgeley;
Media: Acrylic airbrush and color pencil on black card

FIGURE 9.36 Proposed Space Club, a future leisure environment with gambling, dining, and transportation, 1985.

Design and Illustration: Syd Mead, Incorporated; *Medium*: Gouache

FIGURE 9.37 Master suite of a private jet airliner, commissioned by an Arabian prince, 1985.

Design and illustration: Syd Mead, Incorporated; *Medium*: Gouache

A technique utilized to visualize several interior spaces at one time is the isometric view, here a guest room that doubles as a temporary office for travelers.

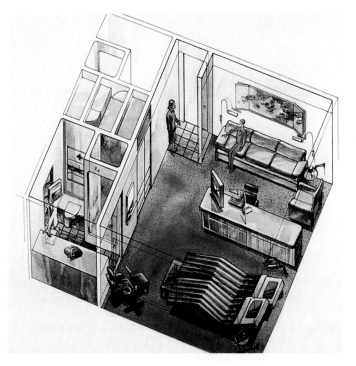

FIGURE 9.38   **Prototype design for a guest room, 1985.**
Design: Index, The Design Firm;
Illustrator: Jack Hanna;
Media: Gouache and inkline

This humorous rendering, primarily executed in a single color with accents in a second tone—not unlike a technique used by cartoonists—is one of a series commissioned for guest suites based on fantasy themes.

FIGURE 9.39   **Eskimo theme guest room, The Fantasyland Hotel, West Edmonton Mall, Edmonton, Alberta, Canada, 1985.**
Design: Maurice Sunderland Architecture;
Illustrator: Thibault Illustrators Limited;
Media: Mixed

Complex ceiling structures and elliptical space represent both technical and artistic challenges for the renderer. This perspective accents the length of the arena and shows the action in the speed-skating lanes and the figure skaters in the center rinks.

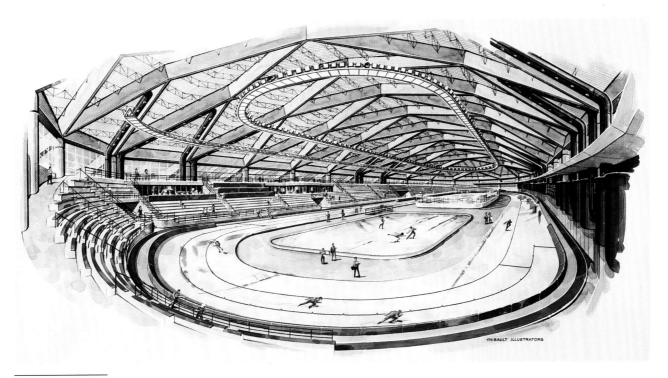

FIGURE 9.40　Skating Arena for the 1988 Olympics, Calgary, Alberta, Canada, 1986.
Design: Graham McCourt Architects; *Illustrator*: Thibault Illustrators; *Media*: Mixed

Paul Stevenson Oles' powerful vision of the glass pyramid that is now the entry to the Louvre Museum is a highly detailed rendered elevation. His textures and tones define the architecture and the intent of the structure in its grand landmark setting. Silhouetted figures, which act as rhythmic elements in the space, also provide scale for the abstract composition of the pyramid and the historic buildings that surround the courtyard.

FIGURE 9.41   "Interior View of Addition to the Louvre (from the Pyramid Looking into the Court Napoleon)," Paris, France, 1987.
Design: I. M. Pei, FAIA; *Illustrator*: Paul Stevenson Oles, FAIA; *Media*: Black Prismacolor pencil, airbrush, and computer-plotted inkline on illustration board

Rendered elevations are often used by architects as they develop their designs because they can give both architect and client a multilevel view of interior spaces.

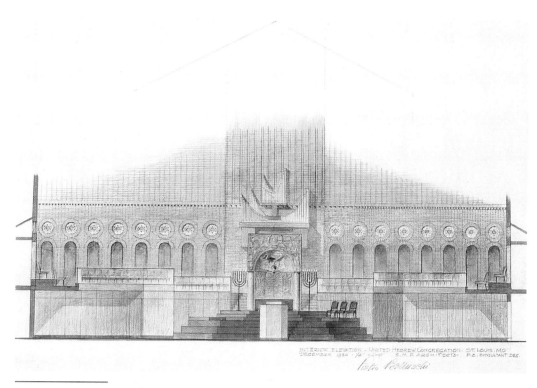

FIGURE 9.42   Interior elevation, United Hebrew Congregation, St. Louis, Missouri, 1986.
Design: S.M.P. Architects, and Pietro Belluschi, consultant designer; *Illustrator*: Pietro Belluschi

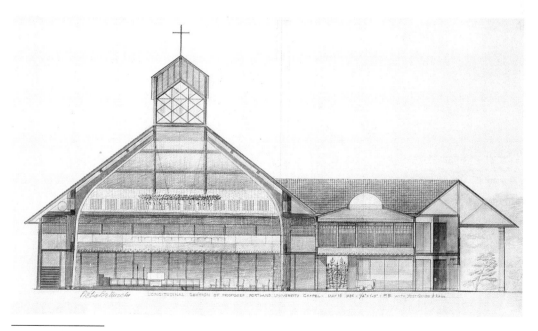

FIGURE 9.43   Longitudinal section, proposed Portland University Chapel, 1985.
Design: Pietro Belluschi with Yost, Grube & Hall; *Illustrator*: Pietro Belluschi;
Media: Pen-and-ink and marker

(*Source: Prints and Drawings Collection, The Octagon Museum, American Architectural Foundation.*)

When illustrating a retail environment, the merchandise and the displays are always highlighted with color, while the positioning of people and the architectural background are minimized.

FIGURE 9.44 **Boyd's Men's Store, Philadelphia, Pennsylvania, 1989.**
Design and illustration: Charles E. Broudy & Associates, P.C. (D. Schwing); *Media:* Marker and pen

FIGURE 9.45 **Marshall Fields, Columbus, Ohio, 1989.**
Design and illustration: FRCH Design International

FIGURE 9.46 **Rivercenter, San Antonio, Texas, 1986.**
Design: Urban Design Group; *Illustrator:* Prelim; *Medium:* Gouache

The display of dinosaurs and the people who come to view the exhibits are the focal points for this gallery setting.

FIGURE 9.47   **Proposed Dinosaur Gallery, Museum of the Rockies, Bozeman, Montana, 1987.**
Design: Mattson, Prugh & Lenon, Architects; *Illustrator*: Henry E. Sorenson Jr.; *Medium*: Pencil on vellum

This unusual perspective captures the interactivity of the fish in their aquatic environment and the human children and adults on the outside looking in from their own environment. Frank Costantino has been a leader in organizing and directing the activities of the American Society of Architectural Perspectivists.

FIGURE 9.48   **Main Tank, Osaka (Japan) Aquarium, 1987.**
Design: Cambridge Seven & Associates; *Illustrator*: Frank M. Costantino; *Medium*: Watercolor

CHAPTER TEN

1990 to 1996

Writing about history as you live it is like trying to view a large and complex tapestry at arm's length. You know there is a worthwhile piece of work in front of you; you just need to stand back and see it as an observer rather than as part of the pattern. At this point in the twentieth century's final decade, the preceding years seem like a seamless mesh, but some trends have emerged.

A 1990s "look" has not clearly emerged. Our decade may not need one. Interior design, as a form of applied artistic expression, may well provide the balance between the revolutionary swings of apparel and the evolutionary movements of architecture. Interiors as beautiful and varied as any created during this century are being produced right now, as can be seen in this chapter's drawings. The 1990s is a microcosm of the whole twentieth century, a time capsule of its past years. Art Deco is back; the 1950s are back; Arts and Crafts is back; Country English is still very in.

The concept of sustainable design is beginning to be recognized as part of the future of residences and workplaces. To conserve resources, designers are using cleaner and safer materials and renewable wood sources, such as wood from plantations or natural forests that are certified sustainable or approved by the Rainforest Alliance. One company manufactures its furniture line from odd pieces of spruce left over from the construction of piano sounding boards and the floor planks of an old warehouse. Other companies use CFC-free (chlorofluorocarbons) foam. IKEA stocks a chair made of recycled plastic. Antiques are reconstructed without the use of toxic chemicals and substances.

Faced with such real-world problems such as widespread corporate downsizing, unresolved social problems in cities and towns, and an aging infrastructure, the public may not be seeking the latest trend in interior design to capture its interest and feed its collective artistic temperament. Rather, it may be just as satisfied with refining what it recognizes and feels comfortable with. That it will adopt as a form of self-expression an interior environment which it can control is a strong factor in making decisions concerning the creation or modifying of personal residential spaces. Commercial and institutional design decisions are driven by different sets of objectives.

One New York interior designer described his current design philosophy this way. "I try to work the way Mother Nature does, putting together different shapes and textures. Think of a forest where there are all these different colors, lights, textures and even smells, but it's still calm and restful."

In a time of economic and political upheavals and abounding technologies, human vision is at the same time being squared off to fit computer and video screens while the human imagination is going beyond "space." *Virtual* and *cyber* have been quickly absorbed into the lexicon. A great deal of human energy is being expended on harnessing technology.

Historians might compare this effort with the Industrial Revolution in the long wave curve plotting the critical path of human history on planet Earth. This decade has made a place for a new breed of visualists. Part designer, part technician, part theoretician, these visualists are creating comprehensible forms not from traditional drawing materials, but from electronic impulses.

The retail furniture industry, based in and around High Point, North Carolina, has long held onto its market weeks, a travel-intensive loop by merchants to view the latest introductions by manufacturers of furniture, accessories, floor coverings, and the like. The next generation of such visits by home furnishings store owners may be a trip to the CD-ROM player.

The quest for antiques (real or imagined), collectibles, flea markets, auctions, and yard sale bargains has reached the status of a national pasttime. Entire malls, such as Chic and Cheap in Los Angeles, have been positioned to supply merchandise to achieve the *neoancestral* look, which when tastefully arranged in one's home, should make the place look like it has been in the family for generations.

Furniture and lighting as art for the home or office has gained a thoughtful following. Most such furniture pieces are still out of the price range of most consumers. However, distinctive lighting creations, which can serve as both illumination and art, can bring a fresh and original look to a living space or to public areas in commercial buildings. Neon, both restored vintage examples and highly original new creations, is gaining a following, aided by the efforts of the Museum of Neon Art in Los Angeles and Let There Be Neon in New York, with shows and publications.

Not since the Quickborner Team from Germany introduced the open office concept with such an installation 35 years ago in Du Pont's Freon Division in Wilmington, Delaware, has there been such a mass introduction of new terms needed to describe the design and function of a contemporary office. There are now new techniques to explain how offices and the structures that support them interact, as in the cutaway perspective of the New York City trading room of Goldman Sachs & Co. (Fig. 10.29).

Work pods, where knowledge workers can arrange their own work spaces, are receiving management support at several multinational organizations. Partitions defining one-person workstations have tightened in 10 years from 110 square feet to 64 square feet. Flex space is in; it's an era of the office-on-wheels. Companies with new or expanding overseas outposts are staging planning meetings by videoconferencing, with plans simplified and reduced to 8-½ × 11 inches for easy faxing.

In 1994, New York's Museum of Modern Art mounted a major Frank Lloyd Wright retrospective with a satellite exhibit at the Metropolitan

Museum of Art. In 1993, The Art Institute of Chicago's remarkable show, "Chicago Architecture and Design, 1923–1993," traced 70 years of design in one of the world's most design-aware cities. "Classical Taste in America: 1800–1840" drew big crowds at the Baltimore Museum of Art and the Mint Museum in Charlotte, North Carolina. This elegant show paid tribute to the collective achievements of the early decorative arts in the United States.

In Chicago, architect Stanley Tigerman and interior designer Eva Maddox founded Archeworks, a problem-solving lab where designers can work together to study design-based solutions to problems related to where we live and work. Their projects range from barrier-free systems for nursing homes to housing for the homeless.

Home offices, once relegated to an unused bedroom or an attic corner, have attained respectability as a primary place of business, thanks to computer hookups and information services such as the Internet. It is estimated that over 40 million Americans will work out of home offices by the year 2010. Just as companies are downsizing work space, more people are discovering the benefits of working from home: less time lost in commuting, fewer interruptions, increased productivity. In response to the demand, makers of office equipment and furniture are tailoring products for use by the worker from home.

Coffeehouses proliferate, often replacing traditional pubs and bars in many neighborhoods, and have once again become a social node.

Regional furniture designers and makers comprise a latter-day Arts and Crafts movement. Filling the niche between pricey designer pieces and mass market, the creations of these specialty firms have individuality and exquisite workmanship.

Home theater enclosures is one of the few new furniture categories to emerge in recent years. Consumers can choose from modernizing an antique armoire to commissioning custom cabinetry to house their television sets and assorted state-of-the-art sound reproduction components.

Traditional fabrics including silk, velvets, and brocades have been updated in luminescent colors and stripes, with a touch of faux leopard used here and there. Consumers are educated and trusting in their own abilities to select products that reflect their own good taste and offer good value. "It's not where you shop, but what you pick that counts," said a New York design consultant. "Ultimately, the success of a room depends on well-considered choices and the confidence to make those choices personal, whether you select from an auction house or a chain store. One-stop shopping can be terrific as long as you remember that it's the personalized details that make a room come alive. Mixing helps create a more timeless interior."

The 1990s may well be remembered as a period when we took another look at some really wonderful things from the past, examined them under a bright, new, sculptural light, and found a mirror of our time.

Jeremiah Goodman's unique drawing style utilizes strong values of each color to indicate form in his elegant composition. Accessories are treated suggestively to lend a personalized and lived-in look to the room. He elongates and stretches the ceiling heights, similar to the way fashion illustrators translate the human form when showing apparel.

FIGURE 10.1   **Drawing room, 1994.**
Design and illustration: Jeremiah Goodman;
Medium: Gouache

FIGURE 10.2   **Living room, President and Mrs. Ronald Reagan, Bel Air, California, 1995.**
Design: Ted Graber; *Illustrator*: Jeremiah Goodman;
Medium: Gouache

Miss Greta Garbo's remarkable talent as a collector is evident in this painting of her Manhattan drawing room.

FIGURE 10.3   Greta Garbo's drawing room, New York City, 1990.
Design: Greta Garbo; *Illustrator*: Jeremiah Goodman; *Medium*: Gouache

A quick marker technique was used to create a full set of drawings for the architect. They were then sepia-printed and bound together with the floor plans for the project.

FIGURE 10.4　**Drawing room, 1990.**
Design: Michael J. Rosenberg; *Illustrator*: Dani Antman;
Medium: Marker on vellum, sepia printed

The artist's painterly technique was responsible for this contemporary variation on the classic room portrait.

FIGURE 10.5　**Living room, "Montague Terrace #2 (afternoon)," Brooklyn, New York, 1991.**
Artist: Judith Randall de Graffenried; *Media*: Mixed

A lively pencil technique conveys the drama of the design of this bed/sitting room with its tented ceiling and central chandelier.

FIGURE 10.6   Moroccan-style interior of a vacation villa, Vermont, 1994.
Design: Jed Johnson & Associates, Interiors; Alan Wanzenberg, Architect;
Illustrator: Gregory P. Koester; *Medium*: Pencil on vellum

By employing an airbrush technique, this apartment takes on an appealing warm glow given off by soft diffuse lighting.

FIGURE 10.7   **Living room and dining area, Rusuna Park development, Jakarta, Indonesia, 1994.**
Design: Philip Cox Richardson Taylor & Partners, Architects; *Illustrator*: Delineation Graphix (Serge Zaleski); *Media*: Tempera/gouache on illustration board

The illustrator set the scene for a dinner party by realistically portraying people in an appealing living/dining area of a city apartment, and adding the drama of a balcony and views of the nighttime sky.

FIGURE 10.8 **Living room and dining room in an urban high-rise, 1992.**
Design and illustration: Interior Design Force; *Media*: Ink and watercolor

Joan Melnick, an illustrator and professor of interior design, used artistic license to elongate the window and drapery to create a distinctive vignette of a small sitting room.

The symmetry of the wall opening and paneling is typical of classical architecture. From this detailed elevation, the designer has the option of using this version as the final presentation drawing to the client or working up a full perspective rendering.

FIGURE 10.9
Sitting room, 1990.
Illustrator: Joan Melnick; *Medium*: Watercolor

FIGURE 10.10 **Living room elevation, Long Island, New York, 1990.**
Design: Buttrick White & Burtis, Architects; *Illustrator*: Gary Brewer; *Medium*: Color pencil on paper

Figures 10.11 and 10.12 are examples of basic working sketches to convey spatial concepts to clients. Such sketches are visual tools used consistently by designers.

Interior Design magazine featured eight pages of Albert Hadley's drawings in its November 1994 issue. "Drawing *is* a design process," he said in the article. "Drawings allow you to define and refine a concept. They are the essential first step in elaborating your vision."

FIGURE 10.11   **Main salon of a yacht, 1991.**
Design and illustration: Geoffrey N. Bradfield, Jay Spectre, Incorporated; *Medium*: Pen-and-ink

FIGURE 10.12   **Living room, Greenwich, Connecticut, 1993.**
Design and illustration: Albert Hadley, FASID, Parish-Hadley Associates; *Medium*: Felt-tip pen

Joan Melnick's loose style, lively brush stroke, and her use of white showing through the drawing gives sparkle to this perspective.

FIGURE 10.13   **Russian-style dining room for a showhouse, Long Island, New York, 1993.**
Design: Teri Seidman, Allied Member, ASID, and John Buscarello, ASID (for Mansions for Millionaires); *Illustrator*: Joan Melnick; *Medium*: Watercolor

This elegant dining room shows the designer's luxurious choice of materials, from the Chinese wall screen to the antique rugs and chairs. It was painted in a loose black-and-white gouache technique.

FIGURE 10.14 **Dining room, Southport, Connecticut, 1991.** *Design*: Richard Mervis Design; *Illustrator*: Dani Antman; *Medium*: Gouache

This fantasy view from dining room to sitting room was designed by Dani Antman for an exhibit staged by leading New York City illustrators. The elaborate foreground leads the viewer through a progression of spaces. Colors are strong in the foreground, tapering off to soft in the background.

FIGURE 10.15 **Concept for a dining room, 1990.** *Illustrator*: Dani Antman; *Medium*: Gouache

Dani Antman's fantasy drawing has a warm color scheme, against which the white and gold lines appear to glow.

FIGURE 10.16   **Fantasy bedroom created for the New York Society of Renderers Show, New York City, 1990.**
Illustrator: Dani Antman; *Medium*: Gouache

The drawing for the Clinton's imaginary bedroom/sitting suite, created for the 1992 Showhouse, Southampton, New York, is surrounded by swatches of proposed fabrics and trims. (Newsday, *Home section*, *September 27, 1992, page 45.*)

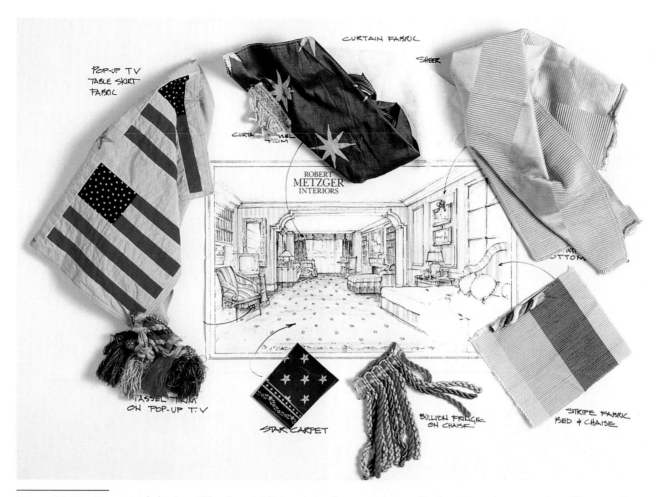

FIGURE 10.17   **Proposed design of bedroom/sitting suite for President Bill Clinton and First Lady Hillary Rodham Clinton, the White House, Washington, D. C., 1992.**

Design and illustration: Robert Metzger Interiors; *Media*: Mixed

This royal bedroom is depicted in a crisp, clean watercolor style.

FIGURE 10.18   **Bedroom of guest suite, proposal for the King of Oman, Guitar, Oman, 1992.**
Design: Norr Architects; *Illustrators:* Barbara Morello and Carlos Ott; *Medium:* Watercolor

The restoration of this historic Civil War–era (c.) home is given a lively treatment by Ernest Wildner-Fox's characteristic loose and energetic style.

FIGURE 10.19   **Bedroom, James F. D. Lanier Mansion, Madison, Indiana, 1993.**
Design: Michael Brown Interiors; *Illustrator:* Ernest Wildner-Fox; *Medium:* Gouache

The visualization of the architectural design leads the eye, starting at the main entrance. The progression of space is aided by the geometric floor pattern to an arched ceiling vestibule and a curved wall beyond. The detailed depiction of the two side rooms, though they occupy a minimum of space on the drawing, adds realism and visual drama.

FIGURE 10.20   **Vie-A-Mer Spa, Sarasota, Florida, 1992.**
Design concept and illustration: Jeremiah Goodman; *Medium*: Gouache

Soft controlled watercolor washes beautifully express the linear patterns within the window mullions. Thomas Schaller painted reflections of the walls and ceiling to add interest to the expanse of floor space.

FIGURE 10.21   **Lobby, United States Courthouse Competition, Foley Square, New York City, 1990.**
Design: Kohn Pedersen Fox Associates; *Illustrator:* Thomas W. Schaller, AIA; *Medium:* Watercolor

For figures 10.22 to 10.28, when depicting big, complex interior spaces such as lobbies, illustrators show people moving through the space and their projected traffic patterns. Wall and ceiling treatments become important in illustrations for speculative commercial structures as attractive lobby features help to rent space throughout the building.

Figures 10.22 through 10.25 are from Pacific Plaza, Hong Kong, 1991. Development of concept, from sketch to final rendering.

FIGURE 10.22
Linework transferred onto gray card and first airbrush color applied.
Design: Keith Griffiths Architects;
Illustrator: Peter Edgeley

FIGURE 10.23
First color study in color pencil.
Design: Keith Griffiths Architects;
Illustrator: Peter Edgeley

FIGURE 10.24
Multiple airbrush colors applied.
Design: Keith Griffiths Architects;
Illustrator: Peter Edgeley

FIGURE 10.25
Final highlighting, reflections, and people added.
Design: Keith Griffiths Architects;
Illustrator: Peter Edgeley

FIGURE 10.26   Lobby, competition for proposed office building, Ministry of Transportation, Head Office, St. Catherines, Ontario, Canada, 1993.

Design: Richard Stevens Architect; *Illustrator*: Christine Hempel; *Medium*: Watercolor

FIGURE 10.27   **Lobby, NCNB Tower, 1990.**

Design: Cesar Pelli, FAIA, Architect; *Illustrator*: R. B. Ferrier, FAIA; *Media*: Graphite, watercolor

FIGURE 10.28 **Lobby, Federal Building and United States Courthouse, Minneapolis, Minnesota, 1993.**
Design: Kohn Pedersen Fox Associates; *Illustrator*: Vladislav Yeliseyev; *Media*: Watercolor and color pencil

This drawing combines structural layers above and below the office, shown in the same view as the individual workstations. Computer-aided design and drafting (CADD) allows designers to make changes in complex designs as they develop and quickly provide a visual record to the client.

FIGURE 10.29   Cut-away perspective of the trading floor, Goldman Sachs & Co., New York City, 1993.

Design and illustration: Skidmore, Owings & Merrill, New York (Yangwei Yee, AIA);

Media: CADD and color printer output

The table settings with napkins and flower arrangement in place give importance and life to the foreground. Note the flairs of sparkle Buddy Leahy introduced on shiny and reflective surfaces that add a glamorous, festive feel to this environment.

FIGURE 10.30 **Banquet hall, 1990.**
Illustrator: Buddy Leahy;
Media: Watercolor and gouache

Light and shadow, the perspective of the soaring cathedral ceiling, and the contrast of the white stone fireplace against the natural wood interior combine for a handsome representation of an elegant lodge.

FIGURE 10.31 **Lobby of the Oregon Golf Club, Portland, Oregon, 1992.**
Design: J. Kattman & Associates, Interior Design; William Zmistowski Associates, Architects;
Illustrators: Design Conceptuals (Paul and Carol Ann Clayton);
Medium: Gouache

Fantasy themes have become an important image for several restaurant chains, including the international Planet Hollywood group. Illustrator Andrew Hickes, an architect by training, rendered this view with cartoonlike action elements.

FIGURE 10.32   **Planet Hollywood, Washington, D.C., 1992.**
Design: The Rockwell Group; *Illustrator*: Andrew Hickes; *Medium*: Airbrush

Syd Mead's distinctive style here interprets a space-age fantasy world, straight out of a sci-fi movie, for a proposed nightclub setting.

FIGURE 10.33   **Gammon 3 nightclub, Tokyo, Japan.**
Design and illustration: Syd Mead, Incorporated; *Medium*: Gouache

A specialist in restaurant illustration, Marvin Friedman has a loose wash style that imparts energy to the setting. Here, a mirror on the back wall extends the interior perspective.

FIGURE 10.34 **La Grenouille restaurant, New York City, drawing created for** *Gourmet* **magazine, 1990.**
Illustrator: Marvin Friedman; *Media*: Mixed

The illustrative quality of the rendered patrons of the brew pub conveys a feeling of warmth and interaction. Edward Bell uses floor shadows to enliven the solid gray floor.

FIGURE 10.35 **Dock Street Brew Pub, Philadelphia, Pennsylvania, 1992.**
Design: Tony Atkin & Associates; *Illustrator*: Phoenix Design Architects (Edward Bell, AIA); *Medium*: Watercolor

The multiple levels of this space are used to full advantage as the focal point of the drawing. Serge Zaleski vignetted the borders to create an irregular outline.

FIGURE 10.36 **Proposed Exhibition and Convention Center, Brisbane, Australia, 1992.**
Design: John Andrews International and Noel Robinson & Associates;
Illustrator: Delineation Graphix (Serge Zaleski);
Media: Tempera/gouache on illustration board

This realistic example of a computer-generated museum gallery simulates the various artistic styles of the paintings that would hang on its wall panels.

FIGURE 10.37 **Warwick (R.I.) Museum, interior renovation, 1992.**
Design: Patrick Han Design;
Illustration: Advanced Media Design (Jon Kletzien, Richard Dubrow);
Media: Hardware: DOS-based 486/DX IBM compatible; color scanner; video recorder; dye-sublimation printer. Software: AutoCad (r.12); 3D Studio (v2); Animator Pro; Photoshop for Windows.

Through the vaulted glass ceiling, the viewer can imagine the exterior environment with a circular tower as part of the Trade Center. The pedestrian bridges and the figures on them provide scale and visual interest across the left and right sides of the atrium.

Figure 10.38   Atrium, World Trade Center, Dresden, Germany, 1993.
Design: Nietz, Prasch, Sigl.; *Illustrator*: Sergei E. Tchoban; *Medium*: Color pencil

Architectural renderer Paul Stevenson Oles has translated the projects of the renowned architect I. M. Pei for many years. The drawings are perfectly balanced works of complex architectural composition heightened by Mr. Oles' spareness of rendering technique. The softness of his technique gives full play to Mr. Pei's geometry of design.

FIGURE 10.39   **Museum of Modern Art, Athens, Greece, 1993.**
Design: I. M. Pei, FAIA, Architect; *Illustrator*: Paul Stevenson Oles, FAIA; *Medium*: Black Prismacolor pencil on illustration board

Jutta Hagen's drawing of this stairway was accomplished with careful cross-hatching with pen-and-ink, a classic form of presentation to create uniformly gradated tones.

FIGURE 10.40   **The Arthur M. Sackler Museum, Harvard University, Cambridge, Massachusetts, 1991.**
Design: James Stirling Michael Wilford Associates; *Illustrator*: Jutta Hagen;
Medium: Pen-and-ink

The automobiles on display are treated as sculpture within the space. The clearly defined lines of the ceiling elements are an effective backdrop to the simulated display at the ground level.

FIGURE 10.41 **Museum of Transportation, Brookline, Massachusetts, 1991.** *Design:* Earl Design, consulting designer; *Illustrator:* James F. Earl; *Media:* Technical pen, marker, and color pencil

Illustrator John Simson Mason, who is also an architect, draws the viewer's interest to the architecture by emphasizing the beamed ceiling, the custom-designed lighting, and the placement of the bookshelves.

FIGURE 10.42 **Public library, Del Mar, California, 1991.** *Design:* Robert A. M. Stern, Architects; *Illustrator:* John Simson Mason, R.A.; *Media:* Sepia ink and watercolor

FIGURE 10.43   Townhall, Brewster, Massachusetts, 1991.

Design: A. Anthony Tappe & Associates; *Illustrator*: Dipl. Ing. Peter Huf;
Media: Computer and scanner

FIGURE 10.44   Sanctuary, Ben Hill Methodist Church, Atlanta, Georgia, 1991.

Design: Turner & Associates/Architects & Planners; *Illustrator*: Barbara Worth Ratner;
Medium: Marker on diazo paper

Framed by the subject of the space, the monetary border lends a sense of individuality and humor to the repetition of computer workstations in a typical banking office environment.

<small>Figure 10.45 **Currency Division, National Westminster Bank, New York City, 1992.**
Design: Gensler;
Illustrator: Andrew Hickes;
Medium: Airbrush</small>

The lively pen-and-ink style of illustrator Carlos Diniz imparts flair and elegance to the banking floor of this financial institution. His book, *Building Illusion* (1992. Tokyo: Process Architecture) contains a foreword by Edward Charles Bassett in which he described Mr. Diniz as producing ". . . beautiful, technically correct drawings in the finest tradition of the architectural draftsman, assiduously researched, carefully detailed in every part, permitting the mind and eye to examine a sweeping, topographical view of London, or a busy street scene, or an intimate corner of a dining terrace. . . ."

<small>Figure 10.46 **ABN Amro Bank, Amsterdam, the Netherlands.**
Design: Skidmore, Owings & Merrill, Los Angeles;
Illustrator: Carlos Diniz;
Media: Pen-and-ink, acrylic paint</small>

This partial view lets viewers visualize a typical business day in the Riyadh Bank, with its domed ceiling and decorative details.

FIGURE 10.47   **Head office, Riyadh Bank, Riyadh, Saudi Arabia, 1992.**
Design: A. C. Martin & Associates; *Illustrator*: Carlos Diniz; *Media*: Pen-and-ink, acrylic paint

Rael D. Slutsky, who was trained as an architect, has developed a distinctive style that combines dotted texture and hatched lines. People are well integrated into the action shown in his scenes, such as the workers moving scenery backstage. Mr. Slutsky's renderings can tell a story in a single expressive glance.

FIGURE 10.48   **Stage preparation room, Civic Opera House, Chicago, Illinois, 1993.**
Design: Skidmore, Owings & Merrill, Chicago; *Illustrator*: Rael D. Slutsky & Associates; *Media*: Pen-and-ink on mylar, with color pencil on vellum photocopy

Rael D. Slutsky's perspective from the center of the balcony looking toward the main entrance captures the monumentality of the opera house's Art Deco–style Grand Foyer.

FIGURE 10.49 **Grand Foyer, Civic Opera House, Chicago, Illinois.**
Design: Graham, Probst, Anderson & White; *Illustrator*: Rael D. Slutsky & Associates; *Media*: Technical pen on mylar with color pencil on vellum paper

The challenge met by master renderer Frank Costantino was to depict people filling a large performance space. This view includes the stage itself, occupied by a full symphony orchestra.

FIGURE 10.50 **Concert Hall at Tanglewood, Lenox, Massachusetts, 1991.**
Design: William Rawn & Associates; *Illustrator*: Frank M. Costantino; *Medium*: Pencil on illustration paper

Plans for a new building that would be the home of the renowned Chicago Symphony Orchestra were presented in a superbly crafted drawing by Michael McCann.

FIGURE 10.51 **Orchestra Hall, Chicago, 1992.**
Design: Skidmore, Owings & Merrill, Chicago; *Illustrator*: Michael McCann; *Medium*: Watercolor

Another proposed new hall for a world-class orchestra received an elaborate computerized rendition by specialists in the genre, Panoptic Imaging. They achieved a dimensionally stunning and realistic effect.

FIGURE 10.52 **Proposed Philadelphia Orchestra Hall, Philadelphia, 1994.**
Design: Venturi Scott Brown and Associates; *Illustration*: Panoptic Imaging (Miles Ritter, Robert Marker, Margo Angevine); *Media*: Hardware: WTH Grace Co. 586/60 with ATI Ultra Pro VLB, Nanao F550i, NEC 6FGP, Toshiba 3401CD, Truevision Targa+. Software: Autodesk 3D Studio Release 3, Autodesk AudoCad Release 12, Adobe Photoshop 2.5 Windows, People for People Suitpeople.

The energy, exuberance, and complexity of the Trade Mart's atrium—people, exhibits, multiple levels of space—are combined to intrigue the viewer.

FIGURE 10.53 **International Trade Mart, Osaka, Japan, 1991.**
Design: STUDIOS Architecture in conjunction with Nikken Sekkei;
Illustrator: Michael Riordon; *Media*: Pen-and-ink with watercolor

Figures 10.54 and 10.55 exemplify two of the several options for visually describing selling spaces. The Hanna-Barbera store shows the depth of the store and its merchandise selection. The Speedo store, a smaller unit in a shopping mall, demonstrates how the entire storefront opens onto the mall's aisle. Mannequins displaying stylish merchandise are given up-front positions.

FIGURE 10.54   Hanna-Barbera store, Los Angeles, California, 1990.
Design and illustration: FRCH Design International; *Medium*: Marker on mylar

FIGURE 10.55   Prototype of the Speedo Authentic Fitness store, 1992.
Design and illustration: Bruce Mayron; *Media*: Watercolor and gouache

Both Figures 10.56 and 10.57 are complex drawings that link interior and exterior spaces. A new terminal has been proposed for the ferries that carry commuters across New York Harbor from Staten Island to lower Manhattan. Panoptic Imaging's version has a quality not unlike the c. 1930s posters advertising the great trans-Atlantic liners. Thomas W. Schaller's deft treatment of color, structure, and perspective carries the scene outside on the left and right.

FIGURE 10.56   Whitehall/ Staten Island Ferry Terminal, New York City, 1993.

Design: Venturi Scott Brown and Associates; Anderson/ Schwartz Architects; *Illustration*: Panoptic Imaging (Miles Ritter, Robert Marker, Margo Angevine); *Media*: Hardware: WTH Grace Co. 486 DX66 with ATI Graphics Ultra Pro VLB, Nanao F550i. Software: Autodesk 3D Studio Release 2, Aldus Photostyler Release 1.1a, Yost Group Ipas Glow Filter.

FIGURE 10.57   Whitehall/ Staten Island Ferry Terminal, New York City, 1992.

Design: Raphael Vinoly Associates; *Illustrator*: Thomas W. Schaller, AIA; *Medium*: Watercolor

For its client, the New York City Transit Authority, SOM rendered this idealized version of one of the busiest stations in the subway system. Images of real people have been scanned into a composite version of uptown and downtown tracks.

FIGURE 10.58   Rehabilitation of the Times Square Subway Station, New York City, 1993.
Design and illustration: Skidmore, Owings & Merrill, New York City; *Media*: CADD, scanner, hand-colored

Carlos Diniz has produced renderings of over 2500 commissions during his distinguished 40-year career, ranging from vast cityscapes to the interior of a resort spa. For the Jeddah Airport illustration, the impressive vaulted space is bathed in natural light, a structural oasis of palm trees and terraced interior gardens.

FIGURE 10.59 **International Airport, Jeddah, Saudi Arabia, 1991.**
Design: Hellmuth, Obata & Kassabaum, Los Angeles; *Illustrator*: Carlos Diniz; *Media*: Pen-and-ink, acrylic paint

This futuristic architectural rendering proposes an entertainment center where the audience interfaces with imaginary visitors from outer space.

FIGURE 10.60 **Competition for Takasaki Astropark, Tokyo, Japan, 1991.**
Design: Obayashi General Construction Company; *Illustrator*: Yoshie Ideno; *Medium*: Watercolor

By emphasizing the technology of the tensioned fabric roof and the excitement generated by the horseshow, the spectators give scale to the dramatic setting and seem part of the responsive crowd watching the procession of horses entering the arena.

FIGURE 10.61   International Horse Park, Rockdale County, Georgia, 1993.
Design: Lord, Aeck & Sargent; *Illustrator*: Barbara Worth Ratner; *Media*: Pencil and watercolor on toned paper

The nine-level, Warner Bros. Studio Store at the corner of Fifth Avenue and 57th Street in New York City became a new chapter in the emerging genre of "entertainment retailing." It is a 75,000-square-foot paean to three-dimensional imagery. Customers arriving by escalator at the third floor are greeted by Bugs Bunny in Statue of Liberty garb, an American flag unfurling overhead, and a cast of Looney Tunes characters at the rail of the mock harbor tour boat.

FIGURE 10.62 **Warner Bros. Studio Store, New York City, 1996.**

Design and illustration: Eric Neuman, Penwal Industries; *Media*: Gouache, marker, pencil

Rael D. Slutsky's drawing glows with a soft, vibrant inner intensity. The one-point, axial perspective helps to direct the viewer's eye to the stage which is bathed in brilliant warm light. Light spills outward, obliquely illuminating the gilded proscenium, the ornamented balcony fronts, and the detailed wall and ceiling vaults.

FIGURE 10.63 **Orchestra Hall, new additions, Chicago, Illinois, 1994.**

Design: Skidmore, Owings & Merrill, Chicago; *Illustrator*: Rael D. Slutsky & Associates; *Media*: Pen-and-ink, color pencil, pastel

ADDENDUM:
The Renderer's Art

Interior Illustrators Share Their Ideas on Creativity, Inspiration, and Technique

Drawing, it has been said, is the language of architecture, both exterior and interior. While the basic tenets of accurate perspective construction have been known to painters and draftspeople since the Renaissance, the profession of *perspectivist*—a specialist who graphically represents proposed architectural design—has developed within the past 100 years. Architects and interior designers who possess the natural abilities and technical skills required to produce a handsome perspective or rendering sometimes prefer to produce their own sketches and finished renderings if time allows. If not, they will call on a perspectivist (also referred to as an *illustrator* or *renderer*) to translate basic plans and schemes into a drawing.

Many of the illustrators and artists represented in this book have a favorite medium or media with which they work. Their selections reflect their personal drawing styles, training, and areas of specialization. For example, Thomas W. Schaller, AIA, prefers watercolor. "The medium of watercolor, owing to its transparent nature, is especially adept at the portrayal of the illusions of perspective, depth and light," Mr. Schaller believes. "In watercolor, as there is no white pigment, the areas of the work which are not painted are as important as those which are."

Interior Rendering Today

As part of the research for *The Illustrated Room*, submitters were asked to help us profile how designers and illustrators work today. Here is a summary of their responses.

Who commissions the illustrations that you produce? What other types of work do you do?

- Renderings are commissioned by architects, interior designers, engineers, developers, landscape architects, planners, developers, and owners.
- Illustration services are provided for publishers, advertising agencies, scientific journals, corporate identity programs, graphic design, and CADD (computer-aided design and drafting) consulting.
- In addition to residential and commercial interiors, renderings depict boats, planes, movie and stage sets, exhibits, automobiles, military installations, components of the space program, and technical equipment.
- Design consulting services available for architects and developers, and residential and commercial interior designers.

- Comments:

  "An illustration can result from detailed specifications and plans, but an entire presentation can be generated from a verbal brief."

  "Architects generally think of interiors in terms of forms, volumes, light, and texture; interior designers are much more attuned to color, pattern, and the subjective qualities of the objects that occupy the space."

Describe your firm's signature design style.

- Colorful and realistic
- Romantic and painterly
- Articulate modeling employing a high degree of finish and utilizing the effects of light
- Purposeful renderings with qualities of graphic design, drama, and excitement.
- Comments:

  "I love to twist and enhance reality. Just as a cartoon often says more than a photograph, I strive for effects rather than aiming for a photographic likeness."

  "I try to go beyond the line, form and proportion of a structure to breath life into it, to capture not only the beauty of a building or a space, but the foliage, the faces, and the feeling."

How are renderings utilized as a form of communication?

- As a sales tool for brochures, exhibits
- As a visual communications tool to describe a design intent to a client or to the public, to convey an ambience, a mood, or to evoke a sense of a specific time or place
- Comments:

  "Rendering is a visual statement of the arrangement of elements in scale in a proscribed space. Renderings show the way the eye perceives volume."

  "As a tool to communicate information about space, renderings are second only to three-dimensional models and can be completed at a lower cost."

  "A rendering can be commissioned at almost any point in the design process: at concept design, finished design, pre-construction, and in some cases post-construction stages. Sometimes renderings are commissioned to gauge a client's degree of commitment to a project or the interest of investors before financing a comprehensive design analysis. Renderings can save time for clients and allow them to communicate effectively."

  "I like to have a rendering done for every project, whether an 'on-the-spot' window treatment sketch or a detailed perspective. For larger jobs, clients expect a rendering, or perspective sketch, even if it involves extra costs."

What media do you prefer to work with?

- Airbrush
- Charcoal
- Color pencil
- Gouache
- Markers
- Mixed media
- Pastels
- Pen-and-ink
- Pencil
- Watercolor

- Comments:

    "Pencil is an extremely flexible, correctable medium, and combined with various qualities of opaque papers, allows an extensive range of tonal quality. It is also a traditional fine-art medium, providing a strong connection to the historic masterpieces of the past."

    "Color pencils provide opacity."

    "I like color pencil for vignettes and sketchy work; airbrush for more finished detailed and accurate work."

    "Watercolors provide fluidity and transparency."

    "I prefer the fluid, tone-on-tone look that watercolor painting can achieve over the opaqueness of heavy tempera or acrylic painting."

    "Watercolor, with all its challenges of fluidity, offers the most effective range of atmospheric lighting effects. It affords a tremendous range of expression for architecture, from delicate, airy, controlled washes to vigorous, bold, colorful gestures."

    "No other medium produces the transitory effects of light better or is as emotionally involving as watercolor."

How long does it take to complete a drawing?

- The answers to this question ranged from a few hours for a concept sketch executed in pencil to 300 hours for a complex computer-generated image. A period of 3 to 4 days was a typical response.

What is a typical size of the renderings you produce?

- Typical sizes indicated were 12 × 18 inches, 14 × 20 inches, and 18 × 24 inches.
- Comments:

    "Renderings can be as small as 8 inches × 10 inches or as large as 3 feet × 4 feet, although the larger sizes are rarely requested. It is more typical to make enlargements from smaller originals by photographic processes than to draw oversize originals."

Do you prefer freehand, drafting, or CADD (computer-aided design and drafting)?

- Comments:

    "Free-hand takes less time and can be done 'on-the-spot'. I use CADD when numerous revisions on a project are anticipated."

    "I employ CADD techniques for setting up perspectives and photomontages."

    "For complex interiors, CADD makes it possible to evaluate various views and fine-tune the view selected."

    "I lay out my drawings on a computer, and then render them by hand."

    "I have no reason to think that fine hand-done perspective views of rooms and buildings will ever fail to be necessary for the presentation of design intent."

Whom do you consider to be influential and inspirational renderers of interiors, past and present?

- Early perspectivists of the Italian Renaissance; the architect-artists of the Viennese Secession and the English Arts and Crafts movement; early twentieth-century pen-and-ink masters; the Fauves; artists of the Dutch painting school; Italian old masters (Tiepolo, Piranesi); Japanese prints of the eighteenth and nineteenth centuries; French Beaux Art designers; Breugel landscapes
- (In alphabetical order) Pierre Bonnard, Samuel Chamberlain, W. M. Chase, Frank Costantino, Giacomo Da Vignola, Leonardo Da Vinci, Georgio di Chirico, Albrecht Durer, Escher, Cyril Farey, Hugh Ferriss, J. M. Gandy, Charles Dana Gibson, Jeremiah Goodman, Bertram Grosvenor Goodhue, Jules Guerin, Arthur Guptill, David Hockney, Winslow Homer, Vassily Kandinsky, Gustav Klimt, Paul Klee, Edward Luytens, Charles

Rennie Mackintosh, Rene Magritte, Paul Stevenson Oles, Maxfield Parrish, Joseph Pennel, Fairfield Porter, Nadim Racy, Richard Rochon, Norman Rockwell, Thomas Schaller, John Singer Sargent, Ivan Shishkin, Turner, Jan Vermeer, Edouard Vuillard, Otto Wagner, William Walcot, Andrew Wyeth, N. C. Wyeth

How will electronics imaging influence rendering in the future?

- Comments:

"CADD has been utilized to increase productivity, speed production, and simplify management by recent advances in computer visualization, rendering, and animation. These tools are invaluable to both designer and client to 'see' a project before construction begins. Perspectives can be generated, materials applied, background and people included, lighting (ambient, omni-directional, spot, and colored) and even weather conditions depicted."

"Multi-media offers exciting possibilities. While a static rendering will still have a place to capture an idea, we will be showing interiors in virtual realities with interactive presentation, with mixed media."

"Visualizing part of the planning process will always be an important tool. This will be increasingly influenced by computers, especially from a technical aspect, but hand-rendered illustrations will always have a place. There is a touch of theater and illusion in good rendering."

CONTRIBUTORS

Academy of Motion Picture Arts and
  Sciences
333 South La Cienega Boulevard
Beverly Hills, CA 90211
Howard Prouty
(213) 247-3000

Advanced Media Design
14 Imperial Place, #202
Providence, RI 02903
Richard Dubrow
(401) 272-1637

American Architectural Foundation
Prints and Drawings Collection
1799 New York Avenue, NW
Washington, DC 20006
Sherry C. Birk
(202) 638-3105

Dani Antman
Interior Renderings
302 Trinity Court, #7
Princeton, NJ 08540
(609) 514-8515

A P Studio
3152 Canfield Crescent
North Vancouver, B.C.
Canada V7R 2V8
Andrew Nodzykowski
(604) 980-8339

Armstrong World Industries
P.O. Box 3001
Lancaster, PA 17604
(717) 397-0611

The Art Institute of Chicago
Photographic Rights Department
111 South Michigan Avenue
Chicago, IL 60603
Lieschen Potuznik
(312) 443-3655

Artists Rights Society
65 Bleecker Street
New York, NY 10012
Katia Stieglitz
(212) 420-9160

Baker Furniture Company
1661 Monroe Avenue, N.W.
Grand Rapids, MI 49505
Alex Mitchell
(616) 361-7321

Bibliothèque Fornay
Hôtel de Sens
1 Rue du Figuier
75180 Paris
France
42/ 78 14 60

John W. Blackwell
238 Allen Street
Lawrence, NY 11559
(516) 239-3170

Joseph Braswell, ASID
425 East 58th Street
New York, NY 10022
(212) 688-1075

Sheila Britz
1120 Park Avenue
New York, NY 10128
(212) 860-4402

Charles E. Broudy & Associates
224 South 20th Street
Philadelphia, PA 19103
Charles E. Broudy, FAIA
(215) 563-8488

Lori Brown Consultants Ltd.
410-1639 West 2nd Avenue
Vancouver, British Columbia
Canada, V6J 1H3
Lori Brown
(604) 736-7897

Yale R. Burge Antiques
305 East 63rd Street
New York, NY 10021
Lisa Burge
(212) 838-4005

Buttrick White & Burtis
475 Tenth Avenue
New York, NY 10018
Samuel White, AIA
(212) 967-3333

Janet C. Campbell, AIA
78 Parker Avenue, #3
San Francisco, CA 94118
(415) 476-3592

Columbia University
Avery Architectural and Fine Arts Library
116th Street and Broadway
New York, NY 10027
Dan Kany
(212) 854-4110

Condé Nast Publications Inc.
350 Madison Avenue
New York, NY 10017
Diana Edkins
(212) 880-8800

Conklin Rossant Architects P.C.
30 West 22nd Street
New York, NY 10010
Roni S. Ruso
(212) 243-6890

Cooper-Hewitt Museum
Department of Drawings and Prints
2 East 91st Street
New York, NY 10128
Elizabeth Horwitz
(212) 860-6868

F. M. Costantino, Inc.
13 B Pauline Street
Winthrop, MA 02152
Frank M. Costantino
(617) 846-4766

J. Hyde Crawford
320 East 51st Street
New York, NY 10019
(212) 421-0669

Richard Dattner Architect P.C.
154 West 57th Street
New York, NY 10019
Richard Dattner, FAIA
(212) 582-4857

Judith Randall de Graffenried
30 Regis Drive
Meriden, CT 06450
(203) 238-7987

Delineation Graphix
238 Bulwara Road
Ultimo, NSW 20007
Sydney, Australia
Serge Zaleski, ARAIA
(612) 552-3666

Design Conceptuals
6645 Olympus Drive
Evergreen, CO 80439
Carol and Paul Clayton
(303) 674-1266

Carlos Diniz Associates
3259 Deronda Drive
Los Angeles, CA 90068
Carlos Diniz
(213) 469-7222

Angelo Donghia, Inc.
485 Broadway
New York, NY 10013
Miry Park
(212) 925-2777

Earl Design
17 Parkview Dr.
Hingham, MA 02043
James F. Earl, ASAP
(617) 749-7982

Peter Edgeley Pty. Ltd.
30 Queens Road, Suite 17
Melbourne 3004
Australia
Peter Edgeley, RIBA
(613) 866-6620

Elizabeth Eve
16685 Neeley Rd.
Guerneville, CA 95446
(707) 869-1830

R. B. Ferrier, FAIA
University of Texas at Arlington
Box 19108
Arlington, TX 76019
(817) 273-2801

Fox Design
68 Gull Rd.
Montauk, NY 11954
Ernest D. Wildner-Fox
(516) 668-5087

FRCH Design Worldwide
860 Broadway
New York, NY 10003
Geoffrey McNally
(212) 254-1229

Frick Art Reference Library
10 East 71st Street
New York, NY 10021
Helen Sanger
(212) 288-2700

Marvin Friedman
17 Montague Avenue
West Trenton, NJ 08628
(609) 883-1576

The Genlyte Group Incorporated
641 Airport Road
Fall River, MA 02720
(508) 679-8131

David M. Genther and Associates
2128 Green Street
Philadelphia, PA 19130
David M. Genther
(215) 751-1060

Ann Glover Design
1811 Baxter Street
Los Angeles, CA 90026
Ann Glover
(213) 663-0728

Jeremiah Goodman
300 East 59th Street
New York, NY 10022
(212) 750-9097

William Grainge
3 Glover Circle
West Somerville, MA 02144
(617) 625-9925

Jutta Hagen Renderings
519 Bloomfield Avenue
Caldwell, NJ 07006
Jutta V. Hagen
(201) 226-6426

Caroline Halliday
350 Central Park West #5H
New York, NY 10025
(212) 865-4349

Jack Hanna
University of Houston, Art Department
348 Fine Arts Building
Houston, TX 77204-4893
(713) 749-2601

Pawel Hardej
Conceptica
6445 West Dempster Street
Morton Grove, IL 60053
(847) 470-1324

Christine Hempel Illustration & Design
1 Ravenscroft Circle
Brampton, Ontario
Canada L62 4P2
Christine Hempel
(905) 846-5289

Andrew Hickes
205 Third Avenue
New York, NY 10003
(212) 677-8054

Historic Hudson Valley
150 White Plains Road
Tarrytown, NY 10591
Burns Patterson
(914) 631-8200

House Beautiful
1700 Broadway
New York, NY 10019
Betty Boote
(212) 903-5084

Peter Huf
Muhlenweg 1
56244 Hartenfels/Westerwald
Germany
0 26 26/76 10

Yoshie Ideno
707 NK Kojimachi Quaters 7-10 Sanbancho
Chiyoda-Ku Tokyo 102
Japan
03-3263-4813

Interior Concepts Ltd.
21 Hillsboro Avenue
Toronto, Ontario
Canada M5R 1S6
James Hewson
(416) 921-8059

Interior Design
249 West 17 Street
New York, NY 10011
Barbara Belch
(212) 645-0067

Interior Design Force Inc.
42 Greene Street
New York, NY 10013
Bob Goldberg
(212) 431-0999

Kiser Gutlon Quintal
568 Broadway, #802
New York, NY 1k0012
Daniel Kiser
(212) 343-0288

The Ladies' Home Journal
100 Park Avenue
New York, NY 10017
Jill Benz
(212) 953-7070

Lawrence Technological University
College of Architecture and Design
21000 West Ten Mile Road
Southfield, MI 48075-1058
Harold Linton
(313) 356-0200

Lord & Taylor
424 Fifth Avenue
New York, NY 10016
Jann Walker
(212) 382-7668

John Simson Mason, RA
21 King Street
New York, NY 10014
(212) 929-3484

Bruce Mayron
201 West 21st Street, #15D
New York, NY 10011
(212) 633-1503

Michael McCann Associates Limited
#2 Gibson Avenue
Toronto, Ontario
Canada M5R 1T5
Michael McCann
(416) 964-7532

Ellen McCluskey Associates Inc.
139 East 57th Street
New York, NY 10022
Nadim Racy, Frank Sierra
(212) 838-6850

McMillen Inc.
155 East 56th Street
New York, NY 10022
Elizabeth Sherrilll, John R. Drews
(212) 753-5600

Syd Mead Inc.
1716 North Gardner
Los Angeles, CA 90046
Roger Servick
(213) 850-5225

Melnick Renderings
7 Great Jones Street
New York, NY 10012
Joan Melnick
(212) 674-7835

The Metropolitan Museum of Art
Fifth Avenue & 82nd Street
New York, NY 10028
(212) 879-5500

Museum of Modern Art
Film Stills Archives
11 West 53rd Street
New York, NY 10019
Mary Corliss
(212) 708-9488

Morello Design Studio GMBH
Obere Donau Str. 69/19
A-1020 Vienna
Austria
Barbara Morello
1/216 36 37

The Pierpont Morgan Library
29 East 36th Street
New York, NY 10016
Charles E. Pierce, Jr.
(212) 685-0008

Musée des Arts Décoratifs
107 rue de Rivoli
75001 Paris
France
42-86-98-16

National Building Museum
401 F Street NW
Washington, DC 20001
Susan Wilkerson
(202) 272-2448

Paul Stevenson Oles, FAIA
One Gateway Center
Newton, MA 02158
(617) 527-6790

Panoptic Imaging
16 River Drive
Titusville, NJ 08560
Miles Ritter
(609) 730-1998

Parish-Hadley Associates, Inc.
305 East 63rd Street
New York, NY 10021
Albert Hadley, FASID
(212) 888-7979

I. M. Pei Architect
600 Madison Avenue
New York, NY 10022
Shelley Ripley
(212) 872-4010

The J. Peterman Company
2444 Palumbo Drive
Lexington, KY 40509
Caroline Shaw
(606) 268-2806

Nicholas M. Pentecost
Interior Design
200 East 61st Street
New York, NY 10021
(212) 750-1915

Penwal Industries, Inc.
10611 Acacia Street
Rancho Cucamonga, CA 91730
Eric Neuman
(909) 466-1555

Phoenix Design Architects
229 Monroe Street
Philadelphia, PA 19147
Edward Bell, AIA
(215) 925-3725

John Pierrepont
19 East 65th Street
New York, NY 10021

Prelim, Inc.
5477 Glen Lakes Drive, #224
Dallas, TX 75231
Robert W. Cook
(214) 692-7226

Barbara Worth Ratner
828 Charles Allen Drive, NE
Atlanta, GA 30308
(404) 876-3943

Michael Reardon
5433 Boyd Avenue
Oakland, CA 94618
(415) 982-9492

Ringman Design and Illustration
1800 McKinney Avenue
Dallas, TX 75201
Samuel Ringman
(214) 871-9001

Riverow Bookshop
187 Front Street
Owego, NY 13827
John D. Spencer
(607) 687-4094

Michael Rosenberg, Inc.
65 West 55th Street
New York, NY 10019
Michael Rosenberg
(212) 757-7272

Schaller Architectural Illustration
2112 Broadway, #407
New York, NY 10023
Thomas W. Schaller, AIA
(212) 362-5524

Teri Seidman Interiors
136 East 56th Street
New York, NY 10022
Teri Seidman, ASID
(212) 888-6551

Laura Shechter
429 4th Street
Brooklyn, NY 11215
(718) 788-7563

Shepley Bulfinch Richardson and Abbot
40 Broad Street
Boston, MA 02109
George R. Mathey
(617) 451-2420

Skidmore, Owings & Merrill
224 South Michigan Avenue
Chicago, IL 60604
(312) 360-4012

Skidmore, Owings & Merrill
220 East 42nd Street
New York, NY 10017
Yangwei Yee, AIA
(212) 309-9548

Rael D. Slutsky & Associates, Inc.
351 Milford Road
Deerfield, IL 60015
Rael D. Slutsky, AIA
(847) 267-8200

Henry E. Sorenson, Jr.
702 South 14th Avenue
Bozeman, MT 59715
(406) 587-7113

Jay Spectre, Inc.
964 Third Avenue
New York, NY 10022
Geoffrey N. Bradfield
(212) 758-1773

Sergei E. Tchoban
Hegestrasse 29
20249 Hamburg
Germany
0049/40-48061848

Thibault Illustrations Limited
61-5810 Patina Drive, S.W.
Calgary, Alberta
Canada T3H 2Y6
Rene Thibault
(403) 217-4650

Waverly Fabrics
79 Madison Avenue
New York, NY 10016
Judy Galloway
(212) 213-7900

Elizabeth Wolfson & Associates
9503 Chestnut Farm Drive
Vienna, VA 22182
Elizabeth McClure Wolfson
(703) 242-9159

Vladislav Yeliseyev Architectural Illustration
220 Madison Avenue, #12L
New York, NY 10016
Vladislav Yeliseyev
(212) 689-8384

INDEX

About the Authors

VILMA BARR has more than 25 years of experience as an author, editor, text developer, and feature writer on the topics of design and business. Her consulting firm, Barr Publications & Editorial Services of New York City, serves corporate clients in the development of print materials and for media contact and liaison. Her book, *Promotion Strategies for Design and Construction Firms*, was given the 1995 Joel Polsky Award by the American Society of Interior Designers for the best book on a design topic. She is coauthor (with Charles E. Broudy, FAIA) of *Designing to Sell: A Complete Guide to Retail Store Planning and Design* and *Time-Saver Details for Store Planning and Design*, author of *The Best of Neon*, and coauthor of *Stores: Retail Display and Design*.

DANI ANTMAN was recently the principal of Dani Antman Interior Renderings, a New York City–based interior illustration firm. A former rendering instructor at Parsons School of Design and the New York School of Interior Design, she has also been a freelance interior renderer whose work has been exhibited at shows at the New York Pen & Brush Club and New York School of Interior Design and whose clients included Estée Lauder, Springmaid Home Fashion, and Burlington Industries. Ms. Antman illustrated the book *Decorating Rich* and has contributed illustrations to *Decorating* and *Remodeling* magazines and to *The New York Times*.